Everybody
JUST
Breathe

thank you!

♡

Amanda V. Peterson

RN, BSN, CCRN

Everybody JUST Breathe

A COVID Nurse Memoir of Stamina and
Swear Words

BEAVER'S POND
PRESS

This is a work of creative nonfiction. The events are portrayed to the best of Amanda V. Peterson's memory. Due to patient confidentiality, every story in here has been stripped of identifying characteristics to protect patient identities. Jack is a fictional name, and he represents multiple patients and patient scenarios. All patient identifiers have been changed. Details to each story have been modified.

Beaver's Pond Press is committed to turning interesting people into independent authors. In that spirit, we are proud to offer this book to our readers; however, the story, the experiences, and the words are the author's alone.

Book design and typesetting by Dan Pitts
Edited by Kerry Aberman
Cover photo by Avi Nahum, MD, PhD, Department of Critical Care Medicine, Regions Hospital, and Associate Professor of Medicine, University of Minnesota
Author photo by Paran Kashani
Managing Editors: Hanna Kjeldbjerg and Laurie Herrmann

Lyrics on page 84 are from Glenn Slater, lyricist, "Mother Knows Best," 2010, sung by Donna Murphy on *Tangled: Original Soundtrack* (Walt Disney Records), 2010, compact disc, track 3.

Lyrics on page 106 are from C. Barney Robertson, *The More We Get Together* (Maranatha Music).

ISBN 13: 978-1-64343-670-8
Library of Congress Catalog Number: 2021921841
Printed in the United States of America
First Edition: 2022
26 25 24 23 22   5 4 3 2

BEAVER'S POND PRESS

Beaver's Pond Press
939 Seventh Street West
Saint Paul, MN 55102
(952) 829-8818
www.BeaversPondPress.com

To order, visit www.thisnursemom.com. Contact the author at www.thisnursemom.com for speaking engagements and interviews.

To the many versions of Jack,

and to the healthcare workers

who fought to save them

PROLOGUE

I wanted this to be over. Here I am—about to send this book to print, and yet the story is not finished.

I liked how I'd ended it, wrapped up in a pretty bow like the life lesson it was supposed to be. I wanted to let it go, to let it fade, to start to heal. I wanted to give Jack away to you. I wanted to tell his stories and set him free.

But instead, my shift is going into overtime, and there is documentation left to finish before I can pack up and go home. Don't you hate when you are stuck at work because the job isn't done? Fuck. Tell my husband I will be late for dinner—I have more charting to do.

It is October of 2021, and the Delta wave of this pandemic is officially here. I am writing down its name, in case I somehow forget it when I am old and wrinkly and can't remember this shit anymore. Gosh, won't that be wonderful.

The COVID ICU is being rebuilt this week. The walls that came down in March are going back up. The red signs will return, along with the roar of the airflow—details I wanted to forget, to put away on a shelf in my mind.

I wanted to tuck this all away until I was ready. I am not ready to examine the memories of this shift, gingerly resting in my hands like pieces of broken glass—clear and hard, with deceptively sharp edges. I am still holding these memories, and right now they are heavy and cutting. They are harsh and jagged and blinding in their brightness. I am not ready to look. And yet here I am, unable to discard them.

This wave is harder. We know what is coming now. I am battening down the hatches of my mind, closing off the parts of me that feel. I am preparing for another winter of rushing air and silent patients. Another Christmas in the trenches. One more round of prayers and profanity.

I am angry now.

Nurses don't like to talk about anger. We are the care-givers. We are not supposed to be mad at humanity. We are supposed to be loving, understanding, and kind. But this is my documentation, and it needs to be said. I am mad. I am mad at humanity for being selfish, for making choices based on individual wants versus the collective need. This unit is going back up because we couldn't band together well enough to protect each other. The anger I feel because of that boils under the surface of my soul right now.

I am also mad at the politicization of this virus. Both sides and their bullshit rhetoric have created a climate of distrust and misinformation that is literally killing people. The mixed messages have poisoned the well of this country, yet everybody keeps drinking the water. Nurses are watching people choke on it. They cough and sputter and die, and we have to watch. That also makes me angry.

The part that burns the most is the lingering feeling that we've failed somehow. Every nurse will have at least one case that haunts them with this feeling, this questioning—did I do enough; should I have done something differently?

If only I had known something sooner, or done something better, or just tried harder, then the outcome would have been different.

I went into this pandemic knowing that one day, I wanted to look back and see that I had done all I could. Like the nurses in history who stepped up when they were needed, I too wanted to help. And that is what hurts the most, I think—that this time, somehow, we were not heard. The voices of the medical community are now lost in the fray, drowned out by the political noise. We can't save everyone. The virus is preventable now, and yet, we cannot convince people to save themselves; we are not enough.

I know this is stupid and that nobody can save everyone. But the feeling is real, present, and unshakable. I want a better ending—a high note to leave you, my reader, feeling good. I want to do more than just chart it.

But I guess this is the reality of intensive care nursing—some shifts are left unfinished. Jack is still coming. I am putting my gear back on and laying my hands on him once again. I will promise him that I'll keep fighting until these walls are taken down for good. I will assure him I will be here no matter what. And when he passes, I will make other promises.

Jack, someday I will heal for you. I will shine for you. I will tell your story far and wide. One day, when this is finally over, I will take these glass memories and display them proudly. I will look, then, at how they catch the light and make something beautiful out of what was sharp and broken. I will never forget. I promise.

Progress Note:

Time: 1745, Day 1 Hospital Admission
Name: Jonathan Doe
DOB: 05/11/65, age 54
VS: T: 100.4, oral P: 114, sinus tach RR: 34,
short of breath at rest, lungs sound diminished
BP: 108/72 O2 Sat: 83% on room air,
improved to 92 on 4L NC

Patient presents to the ED this evening c/o shortness of breath. Cough, fever, and chills x 1 week. Was seen at his clinic two days ago and sent home on antibiotics. Patient is a college professor, has been teaching from home. Son is in college, tested positive for COVID-19 yesterday. Wife's test is pending.

Patient alert and oriented. Albuterol neb given by RT, started on oxygen. COVID-19 swab sent to lab. Vitals stable. IV placed and fluids given. Patient denies pain at this time, will monitor. Unable to finish admission due to patient condition. Will reassess.

LabResult, Time: 1932, Day 1 - COVID-19 test is positive.
Orders, Time: 2109, Day 1 - Admit to inpatient.

Fuck, here's another one. We are seeing them more and more now. I bet he got it from his son, so freaking sad. I wonder what he teaches. Let me see if I can give him some ice water. Oh, and I have to grab him a urinal. And chart his weight. And get another blood pressure; I doubt he runs that low on a regular day. At least he is managing on 4L so far. Maybe I can get his admission questions done if he isn't too tired yet; Lord knows he won't be able to later. Here we go . . .

WHO [World Health Organization] SAYS MYSTERIOUS ILLNESS IN CHINA LIKELY BEING CAUSED BY NEW VIRUS

January 9, 2020, *STAT News*

CHINA CONFIRMS HUMAN-TO-HUMAN TRANSMISSION OF COVID-19

January 20, 2020, BBC News

CDC TO SCREEN AT THREE US AIRPORTS FOR SIGNS OF NEW VIRUS FROM CHINA

January 20, 2020, *CNN Health*

FIRST TRAVEL-RELATED CASE OF 2019 NOVEL CORONAVIRUS DETECTED IN UNITED STATES

January 21, 2020, *CDC*

WHO ISSUES GLOBAL HEALTH EMERGENCY: AS VIRUS SPREADS, U.S. TEMPORARILY BARS FOREIGNERS WHO'VE VISITED CHINA

January 31, 2020, *NY Times*

US DECLARES PUBLIC HEALTH EMERGENCY

February 3, 2020, *Reuters*

WISCONSIN CONFIRMS FIRST CASE OF NEW CORONAVIRUS

February 5, 2020, *MPR News*

CORONAVIRUS DISEASE NAMED COVID-19

February 11, 2020, *BBC News*

SCALE OF CHINA'S WUHAN SHUTDOWN IS BELIEVED TO BE WITHOUT PRECEDENT

February 23, 2020, *NY Times*

MINNESOTA EXPERTS: IT'S TIME FAMILIES PLAN FOR COVID-19 OUTBREAK

February 24, 2020, *MPR News*

IT'S NOT A QUESTION OF IF CORONAVIRUS BECOMES A WORLDWIDE PANDEMIC, BUT WHEN, THE CDC SAID TUESDAY

February 25, 2020, *AJMC*

COVID-19 BRINGS DISINFORMATION WAR TO HEALTH CARE

February 25, 2020, *MPR News*

AS VIRUS SPREADS,
ITALY LOCKS DOWN COUNTRY

March 9, 2020, *The Wall Street Journal*

WHO DECLARES CORONAVIRUS A
PANDEMIC, URGES AGGRESSIVE ACTION

March 11, 2020, *AP News*

TRUMP DECLARES NATIONAL EMERGENCY,
ISSUES TRAVEL BAN ON 26 COUNTRIES

March 13, 2020, *BBC News*

MINN. HEALTH CARE WORKERS
RAISE CONCERNS ABOUT
CORONAVIRUS RESPONSE

March 18, 2020, *MPR News*

FIRST 2 DEATHS IN WISCONSIN
FROM COVID-19; CASES SOAR

March 20, 2020, *MPR News*

FIRST CONFIRMED DEATH FROM COVID-19
IN MINNESOTA

March 21, 2020, *MN Department of Health*

When I was a boy and would see scary things on the news, my mother would say to me, "Look for the helpers. You will always find people who are helping."

—MISTER ROGERS

How do you even write about a pandemic without writing about the patients? Damnit, HIPAA, you keep me from telling their stories, and they deserve to be remembered. So I guess you get my story instead. Because I see them in my dreams. I remember their faces. My story is their story. So here goes nothing . . .

1.

My name is Amanda. I am a third-generation nurse. I think it is genetic at this point, because my daughter likes to make me Google things like "baby with two faces," "smallest organ in the body," and "horse lungs." Or, maybe, I am raising a tiny serial killer. One or the other.

I knew early on I wanted to do something medical. At Girl Scouts one year, I made a first aid kit out of a film canister. (Yes, I am dating myself. Let us pretend my age makes me wiser, mmmkay?) On the playground at school, I wore the kit tied on a shoelace like a necklace. It had alcohol wipes, antibiotic ointment, and Band-Aids for scraped knees. I loved being the one to fix people. I liked saving the day. It was the beginning.

At home, I pretended to be the doctor of the little neighbor girl. I used to make her pretend to have ailments, and then I would heal her. Although, "playing doctor" should have been called "playing nurse," because doctors are not the ones cleaning up barf and giving out medicine—but what did I know?

I was already in nursing school by the time my best friend got sick, but I still credit my career to her. Paula and

I had known each other since elementary school. She was a tiny thing, loud and silly, with terrible handwriting and a head full of epic, wavy curls. We were apart for our first year of college but transferred to live together our second year. Divine intervention.

That summer, she had been in a car accident. When her shoulder began hurting, the doctors thought it was related. X-rays were done and nothing was found. Referred pain was not something I would learn about until further along in school, but I remember where I was sitting in anatomy class the day I put two and two together. It was too late at that point. I sat in that class, shaking as I realized that her guts had been referring pain to her shoulder. If I had only known.

They found her liver cancer on a normal day. We thought she was overreacting to the abnormal blood work found at her clinic, but we agreed to go along to the CT scan to see what could be causing her symptoms. When she came back into the lobby with her father, neither spoke as they walked straight past us to the car. It was a tumor, half the size of a football. We all just cried.

My junior year of nursing school was spent at the Mayo Clinic, camped out in Paula's hospital room with homework strewn all around me. It was there that we were first introduced to their summer interns, and there that Paula suggested I apply to become one. She'd had multiple major surgeries at this point—we were now familiar with the staff on Francis 2C, the colorectal surgical floor. You could tell they took such joy in caring for my friend. It was there that I got to see bedside nursing firsthand, and to understand the helplessness of being the family on the other side.

As Paula faded, we met the hospice nurses. These nurses provided a different kind of care, the kind that impacted the care I give today. These nurses were soft-spoken but brutally honest, unlike anyone else had been up until that point. Nobody wants to talk about a young person dying, but these nurses told us what to expect and made it both real and somehow comforting. They spoke out loud what we knew in our hearts, and I have done my best to provide this for families since. I speak the truth, even when it is hard to hear—because people deserve to know what to expect. Those hospice nurses taught me that.

Paula was drifting. Highlighter yellow now, she was no longer the friend I had cherished. Her beautiful green eyes looked past me, slowly, as if through a fog. I told her I would never forget her. I talked about all the goofy memories we had. I held her tiny hands. She died in her sunroom on Valentine's Day 2005. One month later, I was accepted into the Mayo Clinic's internship program. It began in June, on Paula's birthday.

On her birthday, in a room with the other 130 interns from across the nation, I received my envelope with my assigned floor. This assignment would determine my fate for the summer and would be the start of my nursing career.

I opened the envelope, and immediately goose bumps slid up my arms: Francis 2C.

Thank you, Paula, for watching out for me.

2.

Now, here I am, with thirteen years of nursing under my belt. And because I did not have enough stress in my life, I decided to go back to school. Such smart life choices over here. I am now working toward a degree to become an acute care nurse practitioner and am basically drowning in homework at all times.

I should be writing my thesis for graduate school. Actually, I should be writing my "Scholarly Inquiry Paper," as it were. (And using more phrases like "as it were.") But I am procrastinating. Because there are words in my head that keep me up at night, and they certainly do not come with citations or scholarly research. Sorry, professors, but I am not dreaming about APA format. I am not worrying about references. I am here, writing this out to document this story, to give these words in my head the home they deserve.

Here, I can write words like *fuck*, and if that isn't a win, I don't know what is. Because if 2020 deserves its own word, it is definitely *fuck*. As in, "What the fuck is happening?" and "Where are your fucking pants?" and "I do not give a fuck about politics," and "Why the fuck am I a nurse again?" What a useful word. These words are tied to faces.

They are tied to the noise of the COVID unit: the beeping alarms, and the sound of my breath as it clicks in and out of my respirator. These words are more important than papers and homework. These words make this all real.

＊

As soon as I find out they are building the COVID unit, I know I will volunteer. I am doing a lot of soul-searching about this decision, and the best way I can explain it is that I suddenly know why I am here. There is not even a question. And I know you are probably rolling your eyes and thinking I am ridiculous, and trust me, I do too. But even with my obnoxious ability to word-vomit, this is the only way I can describe the pull into the fire. I want my children to see their mom being brave and choosing to help when things get hard. I want them to see me doing the right thing. I know this is what I have trained for, and I cannot fathom anything else. I am learning that nursing is truly a calling, and that sometimes, that call is stronger than anything else.

＊

I fell in love with the ICU the same way I fell in love with my husband. I met them both by accident, having been introduced to each by mutual acquaintances. I agreed to meet them on a whim. My plan was for the relationships to be casual, simple stepping-stones on my journey to adulthood. I was prepared for neither and enthralled by the complexity of both. They challenged me, pushed me, and left me wide-eyed and breathless. I fell hard for both, and I have loved them both completely ever since. My planned one-year stint in the ICU has lasted over a decade now, and love got me here. They were both meant to be.

Intensive care is the deep end of nursing. You give everything you have, pulling out every stop with dark humor and silent tears. You use every ounce of your brainpower and squeeze your heart dry. You witness miracles, moments of utter joy that only God can explain. Some days are full of yelling. Some are filled with the silence of your own breath. You sweat; you swear; you fall to your knees as you watch a soul slide away. This profession requires all of you, but you get so much in return.

If you cannot already tell, I do nothing halfway. Everything is all in. I don't know if this is a good thing or a bad thing; probably, it is both. Definitely both. Motherhood is the same way. From the second I became a mother, I was 1000 percent in.

I approached motherhood with the same intensity that I bring to my job, and that is not always the best thing. I mean, I kept a log of my daughter's sleep for the first eighteen months of her life. Yes, for eighteen months, I documented every time that girl closed her eyes. "Helicopter Mom" doesn't even quite cover it. There are meds for that kind of thing (which I used, after my second child).

I am the mom that does art projects and chases kids all over the playground. I am in the water at the beach and am the caboose on the sled in the winter. When I am home and with my kids, I am entirely invested in being Mom. But I had always been a working mom—I took pride in doing it all and showing my children that I had a job that I loved. I could be Super-Mom when I was home because I got a break to breathe when I was at work. My job is terrific for making me appreciate what I have. I had days off to myself, and I was able to recharge. I could vent to my best friend or my husband after a hard shift. I could take long walks or go to the gym. I could get a massage, or get my nails done. That balance gave me the ability to pour all of me into every aspect of my life.

In 2020, that all changed for me, as it did for so many others. On March 17, the kids did not go to school. From that day on, besides my work shifts, our children were with me for something like a million days in a row. Overnight, we had to relearn how to be a family, and I had to relearn how to be a wife and mother. We had to learn how to be bored. I needed to learn how to do things like clean the house with tiny people "un-cleaning" as I went. I had to learn how to make a five-minute break feel long enough to not lose my shit. I had to learn how to effectively homeschool two small children and, somehow, also get my own schoolwork done. I had to learn to let go of plans and perfection and to just breathe. That became my mantra—Just breathe.

Everybody just breathe.

3.

Nurses are story keepers by nature. Get a bunch of nurses together, and it quickly becomes a storytelling competition. We save little vignettes of life, a string of human interactions, that when lined up together build a career in human care. We love the game of Who Can Be the Grossest, and any normal human within earshot always gives a face of perfect, sickened horror, which brings joy to any nurse. We also use these stories as therapy. My hardest stories, when told to others that understand, help me unload these feelings and process the grief that can snake its way into a difficult shift. These stories need to be told, because they give us the strength to keep collecting more. This is what we do.

Remember my little neighbor girl? Our game of doctor and patient was all fine and good until the day she pretended to gag herself and she actually puked. It was orange and landed in the bushes behind my swing set—we both panicked immediately, and that was the end of that game. Puke is still my least favorite bodily function. And yes, every nurse has a least favorite bodily function. Ask the nurses in your life which one it is. It is a thing, I swear.

I once had a lady vomit directly into my pocket. Yes, you read that correctly. It flew from her body with the force of an exorcism and made the most perfect arc, like a puke rainbow. It landed square in my scrub pocket, submerging my cell phone. A direct hit. You reach a new level of nursing when you get to scoop barf out of your pocket—barf that isn't even yours. The puke points are all mine.

One night shift a long time ago, I was alone, overseeing a hallway with seven patients. It was dark and peaceful. These patients were not monitored, so there were no lights on in the rooms and no beeping alarms. I was sitting at the desk when one of the call lights went off. I entered the room in the dark, and my inquiry was met with gentle snores.

I quietly shut off the call light and retreated to my desk, assuming the patient had called but had fallen back to sleep. As soon as I sat down, the light went off again. Standing, I returned to the patient's room and called their name louder. Again, no response, just snores, so back to the desk I went. When it happened the third time, I grabbed my penlight, and this time I snuck back into the room to see what was going on. As I neared the bed, a loud snore startled me, and I jumped. As I snuck closer, the circle of light fell upon my slumbering patient, face pressed against the side rail. With every snore, his nose set off the call light. Nurse stories.

I once took a very elderly woman to the bathroom. She was the cutest little old lady, the kind that brought her own floral, flannel nightgown and everything. She shuffled when she walked and only came up to my shoulder. She finished her business, and I helped get her wiped before getting back to bed. She stood up, and politely asked me for one more wipe. I obliged, and as I was finishing, she looked up at me and said, "Thank you—I hate a wet pussy." It took every ounce of my professionalism to not lose my shit laughing as this tiny little grandma just threw that out there and waddled back to bed. Seriously, best job ever.

Have you heard of leech therapy? Yes, leech therapy. As in, we use leeches on people like it's the freaking 1800s and we are playing Oregon Trail or something. Nurses, I have learned, fall into two camps when it comes to leeches—those who think putting leeches on humans is cool, and those that literally run away when we open the leech bucket. You know which camp I fall in by now, right? Yes, I am pro-leech.

I mean, I am pro-leech when they are not on me. I would lose my ever-loving mind if I had one of those little buggers attached to my body. But putting them on other people? Hell yes, please. The best part is at the end when we get to put them into alcohol, and they barf out the bloo— Okay I am probably losing a few of you here, so back to the leech story . . .

The problem with leeches is that they are wiggly little creatures. We use them on skin grafts to encourage blood flow to the grafted area, to try to keep the graft from failing. The nurse's job is to pick out a new leech from the leech bucket every so often and get the little guy to latch onto the graft site. This sounds fairly easy until you realize that the leech does not want to latch onto an injured area; they want to latch onto the healthy areas instead. This is when it gets a little dicey.

So, when said nurse is trying to get a leech to suck onto the end of a person's face, the little bastard might escape right up the person's nose. And then the nurse is suspended in time, as they question every life choice they have ever made.

The patient's eyes are bulging, and in that one second of horror, when you are sure you are getting fired, the little guy shoots out of the patient's mouth like it's been blasted out of a damn cannon and lands on the floor. And then you are sweating, and laughing, and no longer feel like such a leech enthusiast.

These are the stories we collect. Tiny pieces of humanity—little snippets of a shift gone wrong or something that made us laugh out loud. Nurse stories are the best part of this profession. They make what we do real, more than a diagnosis or a set of vital signs; they are a collection of moments that weave together a lifetime of working with life itself.

4.

If you meet me, I probably don't match your expectations of what makes a nurse. I am loud. I love being the center of attention. Florence Nightingale would kick the bucket if she heard how much I swear. My husband says that you never have to ask my opinion; I'll just give it to you. I am an ideal candidate for a martyr, that's for sure.

I am probably not a natural fit for motherhood, either. I'm selfish, really. I mean, I don't want to help you with the dishes or to watch your children. I am not the one to offer to bake a casserole or help you plan your wedding. But yet motherhood, like nursing, is a calling for me. Once I found it, I could not imagine doing anything else.

I want to *do*. I want to be the one on the front lines, giving every ounce of myself to help strangers. If you are dying, I want to be there. I want to help, to alleviate your pain. To hold your hand when you're alone in this world, to make it all feel better. To end my day sweaty and satisfied knowing that I did all that I could do to help someone live, or to bring dignity to death. It drives me as it drives so many of my wonderful coworkers.

We see people at their best and their worst, and we document it all. We are taught to catch details, to record changes, and to feel shifts in emotion. We are trained to make sense of the barrage of information that comes at us and make life-and-death decisions in the chaos of an emergency. We are shaped and molded to bend and not break. We push and fight and sweat and swear, and at the end of our shift, we write it all down and go home to our families. There is a saying in nursing school: "If you didn't chart it, it didn't happen." We document everything.

That is what I need to do now—to document this shift so I can get back to my life. Back to the faces I love more than words, those I love in a way that aches inside me, as if my actual heart could jump out and surround them, protect them, and become them. These events happened to all of us, and they need to be documented *for* all of us.

I volunteered for the COVID unit in March of 2020. It is now January of 2021, and I have worked a total of two shifts outside of this unit. I have cared for exactly one patient without COVID in nearly eleven months. One. Every patient, every shift, every time, with the same disease. For eleven months. This book is my documentation of life as a COVID ICU nurse on the front lines in Minnesota.

By the time COVID hit the Midwest, America was "over" the pandemic. We were not the blindsided ones in New York City, wearing trash bags as personal protective equipment and being cheered on by the world. We had time to prepare for the storm. But what we gained in preparation, we lost in support.

Our voices were shunned, silenced, and ignored. I cannot fathom what it would have been like to be the first to be hit with this, and my heart goes out to the healthcare workers that lived through those first few months. But our stories are different, and both need to be told. Someday, I will be able to look back on all of this and fully allow myself to take in the depth of 2020. Someday, this will be just another nurse story, one more link in the beautiful chain that will represent a career I loved. Someday, I will be able to let it all go. But for now, this is the documentation of the longest shift of my life.

5.

Jack.

COVID patients: the part that no one wants to talk about, and that I can't fully talk about without losing the job I love so much. So, let's meet in the middle. Let's call them all John. As in John Doe. Or Jane Doe. Let's not be sexist, shall we? I am so dang creative. Actually, since we are now friends, let's call them Jack.

"Call me Jack," he would say.

Jack is fake, but his stories are real. Jack is every patient we've had for eleven months. Jack is every COVID patient across the globe. Jack is everyone.

I could pick Jack out of a lineup now, because COVID patients all look the same. Jack is a twentysomething who just had a heart attack from this virus. Jack is a fortysomething whose kids are home alone because both parents are now in the hospital. Jack is a friend's mom. Jack is pregnant with her first child, fighting for two. Jack is a little grandpa, married forty years to the little grandma two rooms down. Jack is hundreds, thousands, hundreds of thousands of stories.

Jack is in my dreams; he is every patient I have laid hands on for nearly a year. Jack is your neighbor, your mother, your pastor. Jack is the side of this pandemic that I am not supposed to talk about, because nobody can handle it. I can't even handle it. Because Jack could be anyone, and that is why this is hard to write. Jack is all of us.

Jack got sick a little over a week ago. He comes in feeling lousy, achy, and oh-so-tired. He might have a fever. He might be dehydrated from diarrhea or vomiting. He has a cough and is feeling short of breath. His family is sick too, but he is the worst so far. His blood pressure is a little low, but nothing scary. His labs show that his body is inflamed, fighting a little too hard. We admit him, and the marathon begins.

Progress Note:

Time: 2350, Day 1
Name: Jonathan "Jack" Doe
VS: T 101.1 oral P 117
BP: 102/66, right arm O2 Sat: 91 on 4L NC

Patient arrives to the floor via cart from Emergency Department (ED) on 4L nasal cannula. Alert and oriented, fatigued. States that he prefers to go by "Jack." Short of breath with transfer from the cart to the bed. Febrile. Respirations are shallow. Episodic cough. Passed his bedside swallow, tolerating sips of water. Voided per urinal. Denies pain except for some muscle aches, rated 4/10. Tylenol given. Vitals stable. Will continue to monitor.

Okay, time to get my act together. This new guy seems nice, poor dude looks so tired. What did he say his name was? John? No, wait, he said Jack. Why is *Jack* a nickname for *John* anyway? They are the same length—focus, girl. I need to page the doc to let her know he is here. Looks all right so far. I am glad he was able to pee—one less thing to worry about. Hopefully, he will just sleep tonight. Let me recheck his temp after that Tylenol, and set his blood pressure for every fifteen minutes, I bet he will drop when he sleeps. Oh, and order a commode for his bedside; he won't do well up to the bathroom. What else . . . time to chart.

6.

I am at work when I learn the pandemic is coming our way. Up until this point, COVID has mostly been jokes among the staff, and memes on Facebook. I felt like we were sheltered in the Midwest, as though the distance between us and China would keep us safe. I am on shift when I learn that we are creating a COVID unit out of what is normally our Neuro ICU. I sneak upstairs to look and am met with plastic barriers and sounds of construction. They are knocking holes in the walls.

For the very first time, I see a unit that will be entirely negative airflow. The engineers are installing huge filters, giant fanlike machines to pull the air out of the hospital. These machines will create the roar of a COVID unit, the sound that will howl in my ears for the months to come. That roar is an attempt to protect us from the virus within these walls. This unit would soon become my home. I stared at the plastic blocking off the doors, and it hit me as hard as the walls they were knocking down . . .

Hospitals do not build things just for fun. They do not spend money lightly. They certainly do not create new units on a whim. Quickly and quietly, our facility was preparing for a storm, and we were all about to be caught in the downpour. And now we are here, and the rain is starting.

We are having whispered conversations. I feel a little like I am shipping out to war soon. Obviously, I cannot even fathom what a true soldier must feel like, and I know that it's not the same. But the feeling of standing on a ledge and waiting to jump, the fight or flight, is there. And I want to fight.

But there's a difference with this war. I can bring it home with me. It can hide silently within my very being and attack those that my heart holds dear. It can snake its way into the lungs of my loved ones and put them at risk. And that tears at my soul. And while my mind tells me they'll probably be fine, what mother feels comfortable with *probably*?

And what if I am the one to go down? I forget that is a possibility too. I feel invincible when I am helping others. I forget that I'm also human, with lungs just as ripe for the picking. I cannot imagine. I would rip myself from Jesus's arms and fight my way back to my babies; heaven be damned.

CORONAVIRUS: CONFIRMED GLOBAL CASES PASS ONE MILLION

April 2, 2020, *BBC News*

WISCONSIN COVID-19 CASES EXCEED 2,000 AND DEATH TOLL EXCEEDS 50

April 4, 2020, *Wisconsin Department Of Health*

WISCONSIN MOVES FORWARD WITH ELECTION DESPITE VIRUS

April 6, 2020, *Associated Press*

COVID-19 DEATH CERTIFICATE CHANGE STIRS CONTROVERSY

April 7, 2020, *MPR News*

BERNIE SANDERS DROPS OUT OF THE 2020 RACE, CLEARING JOE BIDEN'S PATH TO THE DEMOCRATIC NOMINATION

April 8, 2020, *CNN Politics*

APRIL 2020

Increased my life insurance today, because of work. Never thought I'd have to do that.
#nurselife
#thusitbegins

APRIL 2020

Pathophysiology chapter of the week—
"Stress and Disease" Thanks, homework. This isn't stressful at all.

7.

Family time. So much family time. At first, I feel like I am drowning in my own air, like there are too many humans just breathing under one roof. Can you get mad at someone for just *being*? Like, dear Lord, could you just *be* a little quieter, please? Be less, please.

Please do not follow Mommy to the bathroom. We don't need to hear the sound your monster truck makes while your sister is on Zoom. Yes, honey, I can look at your picture—of course we can put it in the pile with the thirteen other rainbows. No, I don't have any more paper for you. Can we try to keep the glitter on the cookie sheet? Not that much, kiddo—*not that much*. Yes, we will just vacuum it up. Oh God, don't let the dog eat the glitter. Shhhhhhhhhhh, don't say glitter poop, your sister is in class! What did you learn in school today? That Mommy says bad words when you dump glitter on the floor and attach the word *poop* to everything? Okay, everybody outside; Mommy needs to breathe. *Whew.*

It is emotional. The kids are learning to be with each other all the time. Hell, *all* of us are learning to be together all the time! While I have never been more thankful to have two children, it feels like growing pains. Their worlds are rocking at the same time as ours, and it shows. There are tears and fears and testing of every boundary, looking for stability in a universe that is suddenly changing the rules.

We are trying to build a "new normal," which is a term that I have quickly come to despise with every cell in my body. "New normal" along with shit like "we are all in this together" and "unprecedented" are basically all terrible terms at this point. I don't know what the hell "precedented" means, but I want some precedented. I am very sick of *un*precedented at this point. Fuck the unusual—we need some good old-fashioned stable and boring. Is that too much to ask? I am over living history for a while. I want the Tuesday edition of life for the rest of this year; 2020 feels like the nursing version of saying, "The unit is too quiet." We have to get used to living the unusual, make it as usual as possible, and not go insane. So, we go outside. To breathe.

Outside, I no longer worry about COVID—oh, wait, that is totally false. Outside, I *usually* do not worry about COVID—until my kid licks things. What kind of Darwinian insanity makes children want to lick things? Truly, I thought I had a handle on my anxiety about Kid 2 licking things—until the pandemic hit.

With Kid 1, I was a straight-up crazy lady with cart covers and hand sanitizer. (I was ahead of my time, clearly.) I had a tiny stroke every time she licked anything. And guess what? She was sick all the dang time. With your second kid, you give up. And they are still sick all the dang time. So, you let your guard down.

Sure, eat the Goldfish Crackers that you found in the car seat cracks. Do I remember when we had Goldfish in here last? Nope. But whatever, Kid 2, eat your heart out.

But then there is this freaking pandemic, and all of a sudden, I have to care about him licking things again. Then Mommy has to have a talk with Kid 2 about not licking all-the-things. This only leads him to believe that licking all-the-things is now the coolest activity in the world. And I am now back to having tiny strokes. Sigh.

To alleviate my impending doom, we disappear into nature. There is less to lick in nature, thank God. So away from civilization we go. And the farther I get from people, the better I feel. In nature, I can just breathe. In nature, I can forget the fact that the world is imploding. I can just be Mom for a little while, and we all need it; I need it most of all. In the shelter of the trees, I am able to let go. I begin to shift, to see the beauty in it, to *feel*, for a while, without the feelings drowning me. I talk to God and remind myself that I am not alone in this, that sometimes, I just cannot handle it all. Sometimes, it is okay not to have all the answers. I am not good at this. I like having answers— just ask my husband. Hell, I have answers for him, also. This is *hard* for me.

ICU nurses like control. We manipulate every vital sign to create an outcome. We are trained to think two, three, and four steps ahead, and to anticipate when things will not look good. The problem comes when the whole world is going to hell; the sensors telling me things aren't looking good are just *on* no matter what I do. I think I am living in the "fight" of fight-or-flight continuously at this point. This is not healthy. Nature saves a tiny bit of my sanity and reminds me of my faith.

Because that is the purpose of faith, isn't it? To cry uncle when things get to be too much.

Fucking uncle, 2020. Uncle.

APRIL 2020

Kid 1: Mom, last night I dreamed we took you on a
family walk and we rolled you off a cliff . . .
#familytime

APRIL 2020

Things not normally said in school:
Why are you *naked*?
#WEEK5

.

APRIL 2020

Kid 2 "lost" his banana somewhere in this house.
So . . . I have *that* to worry about now.

8.

It is April, and our story from the back of the front lines is already getting old. Nobody wants to hear about a pandemic anymore—not when they have their own "needs." I am learning that in America, we have no freaking idea what actual needs are. We are so used to getting what we want; we literally cannot handle being told "no" without losing our minds. I am also learning that people deny those things they do not like. For example, if we just pretend the pandemic is not real, or if we can somehow justify to ourselves that it isn't that bad, we can then go about our days attending to our needs (which are really just wants), with less guilt.

Is it possible to be the hero and the villain in the same story? Because the tides are turning quickly on healthcare workers. Instead of being the martyrs and the saviors, people are now questioning everything we do, because they do not like what we have to say. People are abandoning "we're all in this together," and going full-bore into "you do you, and I'll do me." But that does not work when the thing we are up against is contagious.

I never thought I would have to explain how to care for others, or have to beg people to think about their neighbors. I never thought I would be defending the profession that for so long has been deemed the most trustworthy—now, I am being called a liar, the "doom and gloom nurse." Now, they say I am exaggerating things just to scare people.

Up until now, I questioned whether part of me volunteered to work with COVID because it was exciting, because we were being glorified for it. I could not have been more wrong, and this experience has cemented my passion for what we do. Now we are being vocal when it is no longer appreciated. We are trying to help when it is going unnoticed, and when we are being told that we are wrong at every turn. Now, when everything else seems like a losing battle, we still fight for our patients. Their breaths are real; the care we are giving them matters; and at the end of the day, we will look back and be proud of how we acted under pressure.

Progress Note:

Time: 0925, Day 3
Name: Jack Doe

Patient oriented, sleepy. Moves all extremities and follows commands. Tolerating 6L oxygen via nasal cannula, short of breath with activity. Turning every two hours. Headache, rated 6/10, Tylenol as needed with some relief. No appetite, having his wife send him some favorite snacks from home.

Morning, Jack, my buddy boy . . . He looks worse today—more tired, I think. He's still holding his own, though. Keep it up, honey. Hopefully, his care package can cheer him up. Maybe I can get him to watch some TV later, something to pep him up a little. His urine output dropped last night. Kidneys look a little worse. Remember to tell the doc when they come around.

WISCONSIN DEATH TOLL FROM
COVID-19 EXCEEDS 100

April 9, 2020, *Wisconsin Department of Health*

GLOBAL CORONAVIRUS DEATH TOLL
PASSES 100,000

April 9, 2020, *BBC News*

HOSPITALS CUT PAY, FURLOUGH WORKERS
TO EASE COVID-19 FINANCIAL BLOW

April 10, 2020, *MPR News*

MINNESOTA COVID-19 DEATH TOLL
EXCEEDS 50

April 10, 2020, *Minnesota Department Of Health*

ON AN EASTER UNDER QUARANTINE,
POPE CALLS RESURRECTION A
"CONTAGION OF HOPE"

April 12, 2020, *CRUX*

9.

Easter. It isn't about a virus, politics, quarantine, homeschooling, candy, or eggs. He is risen. I am listening to the online church service in my garage. Snowflakes are falling softly outside, and my little boy is playing in the yard. For this one moment, I am at peace. The insanity of the world falls away, and I see what we've been given, this silent morning for Jesus. If there was ever a time when we needed to remember that He is risen for us, it is now.

I know He's here. He has pulled me into the fire. He has tied me to my home. He is in everything I do right in this world. He and I have been talking more lately about the predicament we are in. About how we're supposed to make these choices. I have already made mine. He knows. He knows why I'm going into the blaze; I have to. But He asks me to give my worries to Him. And damn, they've been piling up. Good luck with that pile, Jesus. You've got a bunch more coming from a million other nurses making the same call I am. Please help us. Please keep us safe. Please protect our babies, our spouses, our parents. Please help us all get through this.

We know He can't protect us all. And yet, we go.

Thank you, God, for everything. I will Praise You in This Storm.

Gosh, this is a bizarre time. But I have hope that all of this has a purpose: to show us what matters, to allow us to help others, to remind us that He is here, to sit here in my garage and allow me to give it all to Him, to enjoy a silent moment of peace in the chaos of this world. . . because He is here.

APRIL 2020

Cadbury Creme Egg . . .

Kid 1: Mom, what is this?

Me: If Jesus was a chicken, these are the
eggs that He would lay.

Kid 1: Moooooooooooommmmmmm . . .

#Easter

APRIL 2020

In case you do not have kids and think you
might want one . . . we just had to remove
the shower drain to extricate a glow stick
that an unnamed child *may* have put
down there.

10.

I'm so freaking tired of people thinking this virus is bullshit, and that only old or unhealthy people are being affected by it. It is so hard to listen to.

I cannot bring you to the hospital, but I gladly would. You can be the one to hold the phone up to the little grandma's ear, so her family can tell her good-bye.

It's okay because she was old.

What about the young ones?

It's okay because they probably had something wrong with them.

You can be the one to pound on their chests and watch tubes be shoved down their throats.

But it's okay because we have super immunity . . .

None of you are fat or have sleep apnea. And you're all just so amazing that you'll be fine, so, it's okay if other people die. That's what you're saying, right?

Yes, this sucks for the economy; I'm not blind to that. But do you know what else sucks? The fact that we are already reusing our masks at work. . . Mine is in a fucking paper bag with my name on it, waiting for me, because there is already a shortage. I will wear it until it gets stiff with my old sweat or until the straps break off. I will wear it until it no longer lets any good air through, until my head hurts from rebreathing my own air for hours on end. I will wear that thing for sixty hours until I am given a new one, to attempt to stay safe while I care for the unlucky ones. I will do it over and over, just for you. For everyone.

But what about the golf courses? They're all closed.

I cannot.

I am sorry. This is not fair to any of us, and I know that everyone is trying to cope. I know that this is awful for everyone. But it is hard to listen to you whine. It feels like we in healthcare are fighting a battle, while everyone else is mad at us for even having to make this effort. I am sorry. I am so freaking sorry.

On one hand, we're being hailed as heroes. We are not heroes, or at least we shouldn't be. We're sacrificial lambs. We are going to war against a virus without enough ammunition, and people are actively fighting against us. For every act of kindness we've received, there are equally negative acts happening. Those acts are risking mine, and subsequently, my family's lives. I do not want to risk my life to save yours. I do it because I know it's right, and I love what I do. But to hear people talk about what they want or what they deserve makes me want to scream. Listen to us; we want to *help* you.

For every one of you that are upset about the stay-at-home orders or are protesting in the streets, you are risking the lives of the healthcare workers in your state. For every one of you that says, "If I die, I die," you are potentially affecting the lives of anyone you come into contact with and whomever they are in contact with. Your freedoms do not count when your freedom puts other lives at risk. I am sorry, but it's not always about you. It's just not.

Let me do my job well. This is what I live for. I can't do this well if you don't stay home and keep our influx steady. Our hospital is prepping for double-occupancy rooms and training more ICU staff. We've been asked to increase our hours this summer. We are already using our masks until they fall apart. What are we going to do? We'll struggle, that's what. We'll sweat and struggle and cry. And we will keep going to save who we can. But by God, help us do this.

As much as the hand clapping and the praise is kind, it isn't going to help unless we can band together to keep our COVID units manageable. I do not want to see these units overflowing with humans all struggling to breathe. I do not want to be there, among the whir of the airflow and the machines, waiting for death or miracles. We are behind the rest of the USA, and we've seen what this can do.

Please learn from this. Please think about your fellow humans. Please think about us.

You may be fine with risking death, but I really don't want to. Please help.

APRIL 2020

News: Maintain social distancing to prevent the spread of COVID-19.

Kid 2: Mom, your arm tastes nice.

APRIL 2020

Kid 1 found some antibacterial gel in the parking lot downtown. It is pink and smells like an old lady. If you want it back, it's a thousand-dollar reward.

APRIL 2020

Kid 2: Mom, is it safe to touch you yet?
#coronanurselife

PROTESTS BREAK OUT IN MICHIGAN OVER STATE'S STAY-AT-HOME ORDER

April 15, 2020, *CBS News*

TOUR DE FRANCE DELAYED UNTIL AUGUST AMID CORONAVIRUS PANDEMIC

April 15, 2020, *CNN*

EVERS EXTENDS WISCONSIN STAY-AT-HOME ORDER UNTIL MAY 26

April 16, 2020, *Associated Press*

WISCONSIN COVID-19 DEATH TOLL OVER 200, MINNESOTA OVER 100

April 17, 2020, *Wisconsin and Minnesota Departments of Health*

UNREST BREAKS OUT IN PARIS, BERLIN & VLADIKAVKAZ IN OPPOSITION TO LOCKDOWNS

April 19, 2020, *The Guardian*

Progress Note:

Time: 0310, Day 5
Name: Jack Doe

Patient confused, pulled out his IV. Pulling his oxygen off, sats dropped into the 70s on room air. Knows self; unaware of place, time, or situation. Patient restrained, oxygen reapplied, IV replaced. MD aware, orders to place on CPAP machine for breathing as needed. Morphine given for both restlessness and shortness of breath.

Addendum:
Time: 0600, Day 5

Patient now more alert, apologetic. Restraints removed. Oxygen levels improved, back to 6L nasal cannula. MD updated.

Oh, Jack, keep it together, honey. He is turning, I can feel it now. Another day or two maybe. Fuck this shit. It is like watching a slow car wreck. I can put my arm out and brace for the impact, but the glass is going to break all the same. Can I put that in my note? Ha, probably not. Car crash is commencing. Fuck this. Will monitor said wreck. Send backup.

APRIL 2020

Every night, Kid 1 has her shirt on her head like a turban.

Kid 1: I'm your bath time genie! What three wishes
do you desire?

Me: I'm not doing this anymore. You won't grant my
wish!

Kid 1: What do you wiiiiiiiiishhhh?

Me: Ugh. I wish you'd stop and take your clothes off
like I asked eight times . . .

Kid 1: And what are your other two
wisheeeeeessssssssss?

11.

Wednesday evening.

Normally, a Wednesday would entail me picking up Kid 2 from wrap care, rushing home to meet Kid 1 getting off the bus, cramming in homework while throwing a snack at both kids, and getting Kid 1 dressed to get to dance class by five o'clock.

Kid 2 would get screen time while his sister danced, and I would chat with the other moms about all that we had on our plates. My mother would meet us as soon as dance was over, and together we would run to get fast food. Afterward, we would get home late, skip bath time, and rush to get stories read, and kids to bed.

Today, we did school from home and went outside to fly kites in the crazy wind. We drew with chalk on the sidewalk. I took a nap while they had an afternoon movie. And then, after a family dinner, we got on our bikes, and all four of us took a bike ride to get ice cream at the gas station. We sat on the curb in the sunshine, and the kids were covered in sticky happiness. Hubby brought a rope to tie to tiny Kid 2's bike to get him back up the big hill toward home. We played with fizzy bath bombs in the tub, and at bedtime, Kid 2 fell asleep while snuggled in for stories.

Kid 1 and I are now curled up watching a show before bed. I sit here while the world falls apart, and I cannot help but think that there are some serious lessons about family here. I am loving this time together and am starting to wonder how I'll do things differently when life speeds up again.

APRIL 2020

Four episodes of *Captain Underpants*, a mess made from Nutella, and one naked kid later—I managed to complete my second-to-last assignment of the semester. One fucking test to go.
#lightattheendofthetunnel
#homeschool
#homegradschool
#atthesametime

#UUUUUUUGH

12.

We are slowly getting into the groove, now, as a COVID-nurse house. I have a spot in the garage where I undress after shifts. I strip, sanitize, and scoot naked into our home. If everyone is in the living room, my husband will holler to the kids so they know to stay away, and I can dash up to the bathroom to shower.

One day, they were all sitting on the couch as I came inside. As I walked into the house, I heard my husband yell, "Shields up! Mom's home!" and the whole family pulled blankets over their heads as I streaked by. The kids were giggling, and it made the whole scenario less scary, and more ridiculous.

My youngest hates not being able to hug me as soon as I get home. The fact that he has to learn this behavior makes my heart ache. The kid-hugs after my shower are good for my soul. After this is over, I am never showering again; I am so sick of showers. Okay, fine. I will shower again. For you. But *never, ever* before after-work hugs. If we ever get through this bullshit virus, I am hugging everyone first thing no matter what.

Hugs mean more right now. Everything means more right now. Why is this? It is hard to explain, but everything just feels like *more*—like life is charged, emitting the low hum of a live wire, ready to spark.

At work, I feel more. Everything is different. There is this undercurrent of activity, everything is moving, planning, and changing. Protocols are popping up. New training is taking place. The halls are empty, but there is more chatter, more activity, more happening within the walls of the hospital. I feel COVID everywhere. In every conversation and every locked eye over our masks. Even in the silence of the empty rooms, I can feel the patients coming. There is this feeling of waiting for the impending wave of hospital admissions. We are all waiting together. We are all quietly reaching toward the wire.

At home I feel it too. Everything just *feels*. My kids, adjusting to their new normal, have waves of this *more* that I am feeling. Emotions are stronger; tears come easier. They know things are different; they respond to the hum of the wire despite not knowing why. They ask me if I am happy. They check on me. I have waves of electric energy and an exhaustion to my core, like I've cried so long that I've worn myself to sleep, but there have been no tears.

And yet the joy is more, also. Because we are in this charged bubble, everything seems more precious and more fleeting. The joy hits like sunlight after a storm, and I can feel the warmth to my toes. All I want to do is bathe in it and memorize the moments, like I'm watching them back in a highlight reel from the future.

It is the weirdest feeling, to be living this simple-but-charged life. I wonder when the *more* will fade. That is when I will know we have made it through this awful thing called COVID. When everything loses its more—its charged light, its quiet hum, the urge to soak it all in—I wonder what will happen then. Because right now, all I feel is *more*.

WISCONSIN CORONAVIRUS CASES
EXCEED 5,000

April 23, 2020, *Wisconsin Department of Health*

MINNESOTA NOW ALSO
EXCEEDS 5,000 CASES

April 25, 2020, *Minnesota Department of Health*

3 MILLION CORONAVIRUS CASES HAVE NOW
BEEN REPORTED WORLDWIDE

April 27, 2020, *NY Post*

US SET TO BECOME THE FIRST COUNTRY
WITH 1 MILLION CASES

April 27, 2020, *NY Daily News*

VP MIKE PENCE FORGOES MASK
AT MAYO CLINIC VISIT

April 28, 2020, *MPR News*

MAY 2020

Mask life. This is getting very real.

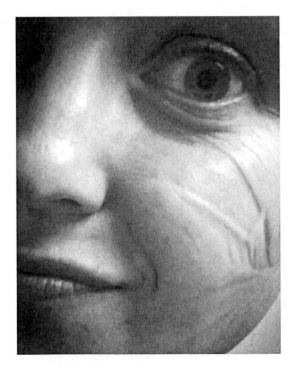

13.

Dear Lord, I'm going to explain this to people until I'm blue in the face:

A mask is to protect other people. Unless it is an N95, it will not protect you much at all. But it helps protect other people.

Wearing masks helps because as more and more places open, cases are naturally going to rise. By wearing masks in enclosed public places, you are helping those who are at higher risk to be able to go out, to go to the grocery store, or spend money at businesses. This is going to help us to open more of the community. If no one wears masks and we open things, the spread will be faster, and we will be stuck closing shit down again. No one wants that.

The lockdown has given hospitals time to prepare. We have prepped units and created negative-airflow rooms. We have pulled critical-care staff from the operating rooms and retrained everyone we can. We are increasing our hours to prepare for the influx of patients. This is helping us to be as ready as we possibly can to take care of people.

For the love of everything holy, wear a freaking mask into stores. We have seen so many asymptomatic people test positive already. And this virus has a fucking *long* incubation period. What does that mean? It means that every single human that you have been in contact with for the last two weeks is now potentially infectious.

This is not forever. I am not asking you to give up your guns or trying to take away your free speech. Fuck, make it an American Flag mask for all I care. Just wear the dang thing until we can get through this. It is going to mutate anyway, so we can only do so much. Masks help. Please, just wear one.

Yesterday, I was told medical professionals are using fear to persuade people to act a certain way. I, like so many of us on the front lines, are seeing the worst of what this virus can do, and we *are* scared. I personally think fear can be a decent motivator (my kids seem to agree whenever I pull out my mom voice). But if fear doesn't motivate you, let's try love.

As things are going now, almost everybody is going to need to get this virus. The vaccines are too far out for most of us, and people need to get back to work. So many people will need to get this. But—and this is a huge, juicy-ass *but*—we need to stagger our cases.

My main reason for pushing people to stay home is to keep hospitals from being overwhelmed. Our PPE is already being rationed. This concern is fear based—for me, my coworkers, and my family. Fuck yes, this is scary. I am choosing to go to war for you, and I only have a water pistol. I am urging people to stay home for those of us tending to the ones who lost the virus Russian roulette.

So yes, I am fearful. I am scared that by going to bat for you, I am going to end up running out of the already-short supplies. I worry about bringing this home to my cancer-survivor husband. I worry every time I hug my children. Yes, the fear is there and that is fair.

But you are young, healthy, and take vitamins. You aren't fat and blah blah blah, and you aren't scared. You don't worry about patients dying unnecessarily because of shitty resources.

Here comes my next fact: not everyone is as healthy as you. And these unhealthy people are not all sitting in a nursing home. They are trying to get groceries inside the already-crowded grocery stores. They eventually will need a haircut. And (God forbid), they might want to go to a restaurant or the movies sometime.

This is where love comes in. As we open this country again, I, as a medical professional, am asking people to act out of love, not fear. I asked you to stay home because I was fearful; you stayed home out of love for the other ones, the unlucky ones, the ones who I will see fill up with fluid and lose the light that makes us human.

I ask you to wear a mask not out of fear but out of love. You will be okay. But as I watch a young man leave the unit in a homemade, makeshift hazmat suit, knowing he's seeing his mom for the last time, my heart drips out of my chest for him. Wear a mask for these people. Let them be the people waiting for that vaccine. Or herd immunity. Or whatever act of God gets us through this. But please, think about other people. Live with love, not fear.

I am going to go into work now, and once again, I will see only the unlucky ones. But my heart will be filled with love, not fear. Because I am a fucking nurse, and that is what we do.

REMDESIVIR RECEIVES EMERGENCY USE AUTHORIZATION

May 1, 2020, *FDA*

COVID-19 CASES EXCEED 10,000 IN MINNESOTA

May 1, 2020, *Minnesota Department of Health*

CONCERN ABOUT PPE SHORTAGE REMAINS AS MN MOVES TO ALLOW ELECTIVE PROCEDURES

May 5, 2020, *MPR News*

MINNESOTA DEATH TOLL HITS OVER 500

May 7, 2020, *Minnesota Department of Health*

Progress Note:

Time: 1242, Day 6
Name: Jack

Patient's breathing is worsening, called MD. Patient remains oriented, lethargic. Orders for 5-day course of remdesivir. Educated patient: this is an antiviral medication that is attempting to help his body fight off his COVID infection, patient verbalized understanding. Replaced second IV for administration. No side effects noted after first dose. Morphine ordered for work of breathing. Respiratory therapist called to assess patient.

Oh, Jack, you look like shit. Breathe, sweet man, breathe. How many times am I going to give this med to people? Do I even know if it is working? What choice do we have? I mean, I guess I am glad that his liver enzymes aren't so crappy that he can't get it. I just want to fix him. This is exhausting to watch. Breathe, honey, I am short of breath even looking at you.

Breathe, Amanda. Just give the damn meds.

MAY 2020

My only poop of the day was interrupted by
a child with a real crisis: needing to know
who has the biggest mouth in the world.
#momlife
#noprivacy
#thatcouldnotwait?
#blessed

MAY 2020

I asked Kid 1 to pour her own cereal. She says she now understands why moms are so tired.

MAY 2020

Listening to Rapunzel soundtrack this morning . . .

> "You know why we stay up in this tower?
> That's right, to keep you safe and sound, dear!"

Me: Man, I understand these words a lot more now!

Kid 1: Wait, why?

Me: We've been staying home like Rapunzel and can't go out anywhere . . .

Kid 1: Yeah, and she's got an evil mother . . .

14.

The influx of COVID patients is ramping up. This part of the shift is the hardest to write about, and will therefore be brought to you by *My Little Pony*. I recognize that I just lost a lot of you, but maybe a few other moms will get me. My emotional capacity is now spent. I am no longer able to soak in any more awful. And when things get brutal, where else can you turn besides a kids' movie soundtrack? Yes, I do realize that booze is also an option, but seriously, when the My Little Ponies tell me it is "Time to Be Awesome," I am in.

And what about Disney movies? Those chicks never lose! When life gets hard, they get stubborn, slap on a new dress, and attack the damned day. If that isn't a solid life lesson, I don't know what is. Or, hell, take your makeup off like Mulan and save the whole country. That feels more like it, really. Mulan, you would approve of my yoga pants. I can do this.

❋

Here we go again. I finish writing in the dim of my car lights. This time, it is on the back of my old checkbook.

I have pages of this life, scribbled on scraps of paper, shoved into my purse before my shifts. This is how I am surviving right now. This is how I document the last round before I start another one. Document, document, document. Breathe.

I shut off the Disney soundtrack and sit in the silence of the parking ramp at work. It is still dark out. I blink away my tears and ready myself for yet another shift in the roar of the COVID unit. One last free breath, and I put on my mask. It is time to work. It is time to be awesome. Remember the ponies. Remember to breathe. Everybody, just breathe.

✺

Back to Jack, who is just beginning his fight. For me, this is the hardest part about COVID: it is *slow*. Everything about this virus is slow, and that makes it the evilest thing I have ever had to witness.

First, COVID is slow to show up at all. This is why we are in this mess. With the flu, you feel like crap within a day or two of catching it. COVID is silent. It waits and takes days and days to do the dirty work. By the time Jack starts to feel awful, he has been around people. He has gone grocery shopping. He has had dinner with his brother and mom. His kids have played with the neighbors. The list goes on. How many people can you come in contact with in two weeks? A freaking lot, that's how many. Too many.

Jack is still in the hospital. He is still on a regular unit at this point. Not too many COVID patients show up to the hospital in need of ICU right away. What's the fun in that?

Let's drag this out some more. So Jack waits. He doesn't really want to eat; he can't taste anything anyway. He is too tired to watch TV. He mostly lies in his dark room, listening to the rush of the airflow. He tries to sleep between the interruptions that a hospital provides. He doesn't get much rest. He just waits.

As Jack waits, his body continues to fight. The problem with COVID is that it causes some bodies to fight too hard. Their immune system kicks in by week two, and that is when Jack starts to look worse. I would say he feels worse, but a lot of the time, Jack doesn't notice that he isn't breathing so well. "Happy hypoxic," we call them. It is not a very happy term, especially if you are a nurse. "Happy" means Jack does not give a shit about the fact that he cannot breathe, despite the fact that I have to give a shit. Therefore, Jack is starting to get more complicated.

Next Jack's lungs start to show signs of COVID pneumonia—his breathing is shallower, faster, less effective. His oxygen needs keep creeping up. First, it's just a few liters on nasal cannula, the little tube you see people wear under their nose. The tube is attached to the oxygen in the wall, and we dial it up if oxygen saturation (sats) drop below 92 percent. Up and up we go, then we switch to a mask. A mask can deliver more oxygen, up to fifteen liters per minute.

As Jack gets worse, we graduate to what is called "heated high flow" oxygen. This goes in his nose also, but now delivers the garden hose effect of forty, forty-five, sometimes fifty liters of oxygen at once. They are heated, because that much air pouring into a person at once is freaking miserable. Moisture builds up in the tubing and makes a horrible bubbling noise, like drowning. There is not enough oxygen for Jack. There is not enough oxygen for anyone. They are all drowning.

Jack is so tired. We added some more time with a CPAP machine to give him some pressure when he takes a breath. We have added medications to try to get Jack to pee off the extra fluid that is accumulating in his lungs. That means poor Jack, who already can't breathe, has to try to get up to pee every hour or so. This is a feat of athleticism if you are on fifty liters of oxygen. Jack struggles. His oxygen levels drop to inappropriate levels—levels that, before COVID, would have scared the crap out of his nurse. Now, it is normal to see oxygen sats drop, lower and lower, over and over again. Breathe, Jack, breathe. There—you are coming back up; c'mon, Jack. Breathe.

WISCONSIN COVID-19 CASES
NOW EXCEED 10,000

May 10, 2020, *Wisconsin Department of Health*

MAY 2020

We are enough days into quarantine that Kid 2 just asked for a snack *in the middle of dinner.*

MAY 2020

The weatherman made a mistake and listed the low temperature for one day next week as 502 degrees. Kid 1 is now crying because we're all going to burn up. I mean, I wouldn't put it past 2020 . . .

MAY 2020

My phone just autocorrected the word
and into *abscessed.*
#nurseautocorrect

15.

It is Mother's Day. This year has been a *grind* for mothers. This year we had to learn to "mom" all over again.

I am a mother. We come in many forms. Some are mothers only of angels. Some are blessed to have heard that first cry, the one that shatters whatever they thought love was, and made it bigger, deeper, and harder. Some get to meet their children later, taking over the role of Mom when another woman can't or won't.

However we earn our title, we all know the feeling of loving something more than ourselves—outside ourselves, of feeling simultaneously exhausted and content, of feeling like we are failing and winning all at once, of wanting to hide in silence for five minutes of peace, yet, at the same time, never wanting to forget the sounds of the chaos.

Motherhood changes us. It builds us up and tears us down, shakes us and shapes us into new versions of ourselves. We look different. Things are lumpy, saggy, wrinkly. We have battle scars and tiger stripes. We have days when we forget to look in the mirror, days where we end up covered in bodily fluids that aren't our own. There are days when we feel like a shadow in our own bodies; some semblance of womanhood remains but feels like a lifetime away.

We feel different. Things that used to matter, don't. Priorities change. Sometimes, it feels like you've lost a little bit of yourself, or you feel guilty if you focus on anything else.

We feel guilty a lot: guilty if we work, guilty if we don't, guilty if there's not enough time, not enough money, not enough date nights, or not enough bedtime stories. If we pick the wrong school or wrong friends, if we make the wrong choices, guilt, guilt, guilt. Mothers know guilt better than anybody.

And God, we are tired. Motherhood is tiring. Not just in the beginning when we're feeding an infant around the clock. The actual raising of children is exhausting. The mental and emotional turmoil is constant. Motherhood is like freaking heart warfare.

But dear God, it is magical. With every fiber of my being, motherhood is worth everything: every sleepless night, every tear, every ounce of anxiety, guilt, and worry. Because this crazy ride is the most fulfilling chaos ever. These tiny minions that depend on me for everything are flipping awesome. They are funny. They are smart, silly, and loving. Every time they giggle together or grab my hand, I'm reminded that I am blessed. And when the sky is falling, and everybody is losing their proverbial shit, it is still worth it. Because life is a fucking adventure, and motherhood is the most wonderful, terrifying, awesome one I've ever been on.

In 2018, the day before my grad school interview, both kids came down with the stomach flu. I was up all night. Hubby got me caffeine the next morning, and off I went to see if I could get into school. I was entirely exhausted and unprepared. There was kid puke literally braided into my hair.

The last interview question they asked me was, "This program is pretty rigorous and stressful—do you think you're prepared to take something like this on?"

I looked at my interviewers, and with an odd smile, I said, "Well, my life at the moment is pretty rigorous and stressful. And yet, I am here. So with all due respect, ladies, bring it on."

A few months later, my husband was diagnosed with cancer. Cancer has the ability to bring everything to a screeching halt, and yet, you can't just stop life. We still had to parent. We still had to function. I began school, and he had surgery that summer. I would bring the kids in to see him, and the healing process began. Every evening when he was in the hospital, I would crash. Emotionally spent, I would go to bed as soon as the kids were asleep. He was incredibly strong through the entire event, but the aftermath of that diagnosis and surgery would affect just about every aspect of life for 2019. We said that if we survived in one piece, 2020 would be "our year."

I don't think 2020 has been anyone's year. Trying to accomplish grad school with work and COVID and two little kiddos at home has been anything but ideal. But 2019 prepared us for chaos. Despite everything that has rained down on our heads in the past year, I'm really proud to say I survived my first year of NP school with straight As. Seven classes down, I think twelve to go. Yes, it was rigorous and stressful. But here I am, and I am still whole.

Happy Mother's Day, right? Bring it on.

WISCONSIN HIGH COURT TOSSES OUT
GOVERNOR'S STAY-HOME ORDER
May 13, 2020, *Associated Press*

MAY 14, 2020:
WI GOVERNOR WARNS OF
"MASSIVE CONFUSION" AFTER RULING
May 14, 2020, *The Pioneer Press*

U.N. WARNS OF GLOBAL MENTAL HEALTH
CRISIS DUE TO COVID-19 PANDEMIC
May 14, 2020, *Reuters*

GLOBAL DEATH TOLL FROM CORONAVIRUS
EXCEEDS 300,000
May 14, 2020, *CNN*

Progress Note:

Time: 0112, Day 8
Name: Jack

Patient transfer to ICU this shift. Oxygen needs increasing, respirations 30s, not maintaining sats on 100% CPAP. Patient lethargic, follows commands with prompting. Attempted to get patient to prone position, did not tolerate. MD aware. Nurse-to-nurse report given.

Damnit, Jack, I wanted you to be the unicorn. But here we go. Jack, this is going to suck. Do you know that? Do you even have enough strength left at this point to care? You are sliding, honey. I am going to tell you that we are just going to monitor you more closely, and that you are here for more oxygen, but I am full of shit. You are here because you are losing, and I get to watch. Isn't that a rocking good time? Yeah. I will tell you that I will do my best to take good care of you. At least that much is true.

16.

Now, Jack has been here for more than a week. We moved him to the ICU last night. He is not the same person anymore. He is so exhausted, every cell in his body occupied with trying to fight this virus. He no longer talks. He doesn't do anything but lie there and try to breathe.

We try to get Jack to lie on his belly. Lying upside down opens up more surface area in your lungs, Jack. Lying upside down will help you, Jack. Lying upside down might save you, Jack—please, just for an hour?

What is it about COVID that makes it so hard to understand that lying on their belly would help them feel better? Oh, wait, they cannot fucking breathe. Yes, I forgot. That does make it harder.

One hour, Jack, let me help you. Move the tubes over, switch your heart monitor patches to your back. Here—have another pillow, you can do this. You can do this, Jack. Breathe, honey. Please breathe.

He can't breathe. Nobody can breathe. It's time. It has been two weeks in the hospital now. Jack is getting confused. Maybe it is from the lack of oxygen, maybe it is delirium from being here so long, maybe it is something else.

He no longer knows who we are. His family is calling us, worried that he is getting worse. Sorry, family, Jack is just starting this fight. No, I can't tell you what will happen. No, I don't have good news. We just have to wait and see. More waiting. So much waiting.

We are going to put him on a ventilator to help him breathe. I know, I am so sorry. We are here for him, I promise. We will give him medicine to make him sleepy before we do anything. Then we will paralyze him, so his body doesn't fight the machine's breaths, given shallow and fast to compensate for his stiff lungs. We will put special lines in him first—one in his artery will measure his blood pressure at all times. One will be a fancy IV so we can give him all the medicine possible to help him fight this. He will probably need medicine to keep his blood pressure up. He will need medicine for pain, for sedation, steroids to help fight the inflammation, a catheter to collect his pee—yes, I will tell him that you love him. I will tell him that you called, and that his granddaughter made him a card. I will tell him. I tell him. He looks at me blankly. Breathe, Jack.

Once the breathing tube is in, we get ready to flip him. Sorry, Jack, you can lie on your belly better now. We put padded stickers on his knees. We have these pillows that I swear are made of Silly Putty—we use these to prop up his hips and chest. They mold to the curves of his body and attempt to protect his skin for the next sixteen hours while he lies on his stomach. We unhook his catheter to run the tube between his legs so it doesn't make a tube mark on his skin, or worse, burrow its way into his penis. No, I don't want to talk about it. We put a pad over him and a new sheet on top. The team gathers, and Jack is ready to flip. We roll the sheets up together, with Jack in between, like an overly complicated burrito. The Chipotle method. Yes, I just made that name up.

One, two, three, and we flip. The respiratory therapist has Jack's head and makes sure we protect his airway. Three or four nurses flip the human-burrito over, while watching all his lines and vitals. The ICU doctor is here in case the tube slips, or Jack tries to die, or any other fun complication occurs, as they sometimes do when we have to play merry-go-round with a critically ill human. Now he is upside down, head turned hard to one side, one arm up like he is swimming. We quickly hook him back up to the monitors and hope that he holds on.

Hold on, Jack. Just breathe, Jack.

MAY 2020

Kid 2 is currently crying because he cannot switch his fish to a new fishbowl. He does not have a fish. #momlife

MAY 2020

Ordered a photo book for part of Hubby's Father's Day gift. It came and the cover is on upside down. Seems accurate for 2020. Keeping it.

MAY 2020

On the TV:

> "The more we get together, together,
> together, the happier we'll be."

Kid 1: Well, that's a terrible song for right now.

Me: Wha—oh, dang, you're right.

17.

Open letter to hospital administration:

You don't know me. I've been a nurse here for a while, nearly thirteen years, I think. I've never met you, and yet there have been many times that I've put everything I have into what I do here. I work in one of your ICUs. I started here when I was green and starry-eyed, eager to learn, and eager to feel. Within these walls, I've learned what it means to be a nurse.

Sometimes, it's loud and intense, the cacophony of beeping machines and blurred voices as we pile into a room for a code. Everybody moving, doing, a symphony of coordinated bodies—the dance we do best. The raw feeling of CPR under my gloved hands, tiny pops of bones in the rib cage, pounding a life back into this world. The awe of the first unassisted breath, sweat running down my back—we all pause and watch the monitor to see if we've pulled them back from the light.

Sometimes, it is silent. Me, alone in a room, the glow of machinery, the quiet blankets of a sedated patient—too sick to be awake, too sick for me to see who they are, to see them smile. In these moments, I'm at peace with my anonymity, working quietly around them. They will never see my face, and yet, I'll work diligently to try to get them home to the people I see in the photographs taped to their care boards.

And sometimes, it is still. Holding a cold hand in my own, feeling the frail skin, the thready pulse flitting in their neck, breaths shallow and uneven. Telling them in my heart that it's okay to go, that they are not alone. I am here with them. I watch, and it fills me to my core, knowing that I can give them peace, comfort. It helps me appreciate my own life, my own people. Watching death helps me live.

The H1N1 year is cemented in my heart forever. Units filled with purple RotoProne beds, lives literally hanging in the balance of God and the nurses. We worked hard to save people, to give them time to heal from the ARDS ravaging their lungs. The one that I still see in my mind: "Please watch out for my mother, she's going to worry," as we put them on the ventilator. Pink froth spewed from the tube. And her mom was right to worry. They never spoke again.

And now here we are, in the most historic fight of our careers. Once again, the units are filling with people unable to breathe. Once again, we are being called to the bedside. We are here, with new gear, fighting a virus we are still learning about. We are now the nurse and the family, as our patients are alone. We are sweaty and short of breath and here, trying to keep us afloat as the numbers increase. All the while knowing that we are potentially bringing this home. Breathing in the silent problem, to exhale its way to my children and husband. And yet we are here.

We deserve your support. We deserve to know that in this business of helping people, that you are willing to help the people helping you. You don't know me, but you should. Because we are the heart of your business. And business, sadly, is booming.

THE DEATH OF GEORGE FLOYD:
WHAT VIDEO AND OTHER RECORDS SHOW
ABOUT HIS FINAL MINUTES

May 25, 2020, Washington Post

PROTESTS ERUPT IN CITIES ACROSS
THE US, AND WORLDWIDE IN RESPONSE
TO THE DEATH OF GEORGE FLOYD

May 26, 2020, *The Guardian*

MINNEAPOLIS MAYOR FREY:
CHARGE COP WHO RESTRAINED FLOYD;
STATE LEADERS VOW ACTION

May 27, 2020, *MPR News*

LOOTED AND SMOLDERING, "LAKE STREET,
THE GREAT STREET" BRACES FOR MORE

May 28, 2020, *MPR News*

**WEARY FROM LOOTING AND ARSON,
SOUTH MINNEAPOLIS ASKS:
WHERE ARE THE POLICE?**

May 29, 2020, *MPR News*

**NATIONAL GUARD ACTIVATED IN SEVERAL
STATES, INCLUDING MINNESOTA.
TROOPS RIDING THROUGH THE STREETS
IN MILITARY VEHICLES**

May 30, 2020, *NPR*

**MINNESOTA DEATH TOLL FROM COVID-19
EXCEEDS 1,000**

May 30, 2020, *Minnesota Department of Health*

18.

It is Memorial Day weekend, and I feel like I am living in an alternate universe. The news has exploded with the death of George Floyd, and the Twin Cities are now being thrust into the national spotlight. The outrage over racial injustice is hitting fever pitch, and people have filled the streets. The political divide is ripping wider, and long-overdue conversations are being had via fire, violence, and protest.

Meanwhile, we still have a casual pandemic going on. It is hard for me to even take in the violence and civil unrest, only because my tank is already so full. All I know right now is that this is adding another layer of chaos into life, and I cannot absorb any more. I am struggling mentally with the groups of people on TV. I am struggling with people not taking COVID seriously. I can't watch the news without thinking that all of this is going to bring more patients into the roar of our unit. I understand that this is bigger than a virus for so many, but as a nurse, it is hard for me to handle both. I just want everyone to stay home and get along and stop creating situations that are an epidemiological nightmare. Again, I know how ridiculous that sounds. But it is all I can think about at this point.

Once again, I am taking to the forest with our children. I am running away from talk of race, of injustice, of police, of anything outside the bubble of my family. I am afraid for the future. I am afraid for the choices that I made to fight this virus. I am afraid to get too invested, as I know I only have so much left to give, and I have to preserve what little sanity I have left. I do not have the answers for this. All I know is that if it is a choice between love and hate, to always choose love. Love can get you through just about anything. And when the world burns orange and the talk is all red and blue, we escape to where it's green. Where we can breathe without a mask, where there are no people and no hate. Where, for one second, I can feel like we are free from the ugly in this world. Prayers for this poor man's family, prayers for everyone out there suffering, prayers for the good people in uniform, prayers for us all. God help us.

Back at work, I feel oddly disconnected from the chaos unfolding live on my computer screen, the cities around me in flames. Inside the hospital walls, the other fight is still raging, one that I can't help but think will be exacerbated by the huge groups of people that have gathered these past few days. My heart hurts for humanity right now. In here, there is just the noise of the negative airflow and the beeps of machines, yet outside, there is hate and fear and fire.

I am sorry. I am so sorry for everyone tonight. I am so sorry that we as humans have let it get here. That we couldn't do better for our fellow man. That people feel so helpless and so angry that this feels like their only way to bring these problems to attention. That love isn't what we teach first, and what we teach most. Why is love so hard? Please, God, forgive us.

JUNE 2020

Thirty-eight hours out of seventy-two in an N95 mask, and I didn't pass out. So, I think it's safe for you to wear one to get groceries.
#goodtest
#nightshiftweekend
#butwithnationalguard

JUNE 2020

Kid 1: Mama, who did you fix yesterday?

Me: Well, I took care of some people who had trouble with their lungs and their kidneys.

Kid 1: Were they old?

Me: Yeah, they were pretty old. Why?

Kid 1: Well, then you should not call them KID-neys. They are GROWN-UPneys.

Me: [*snort*] I am on it.

Progress Note:

Time: 1430, Day 13
Name: Jack, always Jack
VS: T 99 oral, P: 123, BP: 117/71, left arterial line
O2 Sat: 91% on Ventilator, 90% and PEEP of 16, supine

Patient's P:F ratio remains under 150, MD called to prone. Tolerating paralytic, sedation, blood pressure support. Tube feedings started. Kidney function worse, no urine output this shift. Renal consult ordered.

Jack, in my head, I am considering you already dead. Is that wrong? I think it is a coping mechanism. You are just a body now, albeit one that I watch very closely. You are a set of numbers. I cannot think about you teaching your students or connect you to the worried wife that calls to check in. You cannot be a real human, with a life to get back to. There are so many of you that we get to know and pour our hearts into, just to end up like this. I cannot think about the real you. You need me to function, to be at my best. So, I can't think of you as a person right now. I am sorry about that. That is my confession. No more emotions are allowed here. Not yet. I am too busy trying to save you, for you to be you right now.

19.

Jack will be back and forth on his belly for days, and sometimes weeks, before we run out of straws. More waiting. So much waiting. Breathe, Jack. His kidneys are struggling; we dry them out trying to help his lungs. So now he swells, filling with fluid that is not coming out. He is unrecognizable compared to the pictures his family sent in. His eyes are swollen shut, his lips protrude and get sores on them from lying on his face for hours on end. His hands feel taut. His skin is looking rough now—angry ulcers have developed at pressure points from lying still. We try to protect him, but breathing takes precedence over skin. Sometimes, the areas turn black. That isn't good. We are trying to help you, Jack.

Sometimes the pressure needed to fill his lungs is too much, and he literally pops a hole in one. This should be high on the list of "Things You Never Want to Have Happen to You." You don't have a list like this? You should. An ICU nurse has a pretty long list. COVID is on this list now.

Jack's breathing looks worse. We can't hear any breaths on one side. An x-ray confirms what is called a *pneumothorax*, and that means more trouble for Jack. Now he gets a chest tube to help reinflate his lung. Or lungs. That is extra fun. Then, poor Jack can barely turn at all, and the skin situation gets even more dramatic.

Let's add in some dialysis once his kidneys get worse. The continuous dialysis machine is seriously the bane of my existence. If you even *think* too hard about a CRRT machine, it will beep at you. I am not kidding. This limits even more Jack's ability to be moved. Now we need Jack to breathe, remember how to make urine, mend his punctured lung, repair his rotting skin, and attempt to protect his brain and every other organ while he works on that list. It is not an ideal task. So, while we wait for this Jack to heal, let's keep talking about COVID . . .

COVID is awful because it is creative in all the ways it tries to kill you. It doesn't just cause pneumonia, although that alone is terrible enough. Nope, with COVID you also clot. You clot even when we are trying to keep you from clotting. Jack might call you into his room and tell you his foot is numb and tingling. You are scared to look under the blanket, because Jack had been doing so much better, and you know what is coming.

Jack, your oxygen looks good today. Jack, you actually got to eat breakfast; I am so happy for you! And then you look under the blanket. His foot is dark and cold. Fuck. He looks at you. Am I okay? No, Jack, you aren't okay. Fuck no, fuck this, fuck everything—I am sorry, Jack. Clots, everywhere. Clots in his veins, clots in his arteries. Jack might lose his leg. Jack might have a heart attack. Jack might have his kidneys fail. Fucking everything clots.

Imagine waking up Jack after two weeks on the ventilator. You are so proud of him; you cannot wait to tell his family that he is doing better. You finally get to pass on some good news. You decrease his sedation and squeeze his hands. Open your eyes for me, Jack. Wake up, honey. Wake up. And then his eyes open. Only they are not looking at you. They are rolled up high, with so much white showing. You can only see the bottoms of his irises. No, no, no, no, Jack! Damnit, *no*. Please, *God*, no. COVID makes you clot. Sometimes Jack clots his brain.

Jack doesn't always clot, though. We put everyone on blood thinners now to help prevent the clots. But sometimes the blood thinners work so well that he bleeds instead. Jack will ooze blood out of his mouth and nose when he is upside down. His pee will turn pink, then rosy, then red. His fancy IV line will bleed, covered in gauze, the red slowly collecting in a dark circle, getting onto the sheets. Or, he will bleed in worse places, on the inside. Suddenly red stool will pour out of him, blood pressure dropping, the bleeding hidden until too late. Or, Jack will make it off the ventilator, ready to work on going home, and then stop answering your questions. He will struggle to breathe again, and the CT scan shows bleeding in his brain. We cannot win. Jack keeps losing.

Jack can get a fever of 107 degrees. He can vomit in his CPAP mask and drown. He can just quit trying—pulling off his oxygen over and over, screaming that he wants to die. That is one of the hardest things to witness in all of this awful. Jack will withdraw, losing any will to fight. He will lie there for days doing nothing but breathing, and the person you saw when he first came in is already gone. He will pull off his mask, and the numbers will start to drop as he looks at you and slowly turns gray as you beg him to let you put it back on. The monitors start clanging as his oxygen drops lower and lower, and we are calling the doctor, and you are on your knees begging him to give you ten minutes, just ten minutes to get the doctor to talk to him. To please not give up like this, to please keep fighting, to please, for-the-love-of-God breathe.

COVID can find a million ways to make Jack suffer. Jack is who keeps me here fighting. He is why I have tried so hard to get people to understand what we are going through. He is why I am here writing this down. He is one of us, many of us, all of us. Over and over, Jack keeps showing up.

We fight so hard to save them. And then it is time for me to go, and Jack now follows me home. He is with me on my drive, trying to shake off the emotion of the day. Jack is on the news. States fighting about what to keep open, what to keep closed. He is why I cannot talk about politics right now. He is in every public conversation and every Facebook argument. He is everywhere. He is why, when I cross the border into Wisconsin, I struggle to stay sane. Because Jack is with me, driving past the open bars, people lined up in the streets to go inside.

I want to scream. I want to run down the streets in my COVID-covered scrubs and hug people, to watch them back away from me in my hospital gear. That would go well. I want to go into the bars and tell everyone about my day. I want to watch them squirm, to be uncomfortable. I want them to see what I see. I want them to take Jack home. I want them to try to live with him in every thought and every dream. I am angry and exhausted and broken.

Is it possible to hate humanity at the same time we are trying to save it? This is the kind of crazy that I recognize is not going to get me anywhere, and yet it is here. I am offi-cially losing it. I glare at people who aren't wearing masks. I email school board members, town council members, any-one I can think of to listen to my story, to explain that this is real and coming and awful. I am trying so freaking hard to make people understand, and I feel like we are fighting a war alone. I cannot stop, Jack needs me. I cannot give up, I cannot leave him.

I go home and the news is on. I cannot talk about my day. I cannot bring Jack into our house. Nobody wants to hear it; everybody is trying to cope enough already. Jack is too much. I feel alone and exhausted. My family needs me and needs me to be whole. I try to put Jack away for now. But he is here, beneath the surface, challenging my focus. He is here, baiting me to fight, keeping me from sleep, ever present in the back of my mind.

I shower. I get those after-shower hugs. I go back to be-ing Mommy. I go back to Disney movies. I go back into na-ture. Away from the noise of the world, away from politics, away from my fears, to breathe. *Just breathe,* I tell myself. *Just breathe.*

**FLOYD KILLING: 2ND-DEGREE MURDER
COUNT FOR CHAUVIN;
3 OTHER EX-COPS CHARGED**

June 3, 2020, *MPR News*

**SHARPTON AT GEORGE FLOYD'S
MINNEAPOLIS MEMORIAL SERVICE:
"GET YOUR KNEE OFF OUR NECKS"**

June 4, 2020, *MPR News*

**U.S. HITS 2 MILLION CORONAVIRUS CASES
AS MANY STATES SEE A SURGE OF PATIENTS**

June 10, 2020, *NPR*

**GLOBAL CORONAVIRUS CASES
PASS 8 MILLION AS OUTBREAK EXPANDS
IN LATIN AMERICA**

June 15, 2020, *NBC*

JUNE 2020

I would like to report a death secondary
to coronavirus . . . RIP Fitbit.
#toomuchwashing
#nowmystepsdontcount

JUNE 2020

Got my respirator. Just when COVID life was getting a little mundane, they shake it up.
#soundslikeDarthVader
#respiratorlife
#sureitsjustliketheflu

20.

Yesterday, I was told I shouldn't share close-up pictures of myself in my respirator because they are "scary" and "uncomfortable." I should show a picture of just the respirator, or a picture that is zoomed out so you cannot see my face. I can't stop thinking about it. And since I have very little filter (hopefully my respirator has a better one), here I am writing again.

Guess what? I write about this stuff because it is uncomfortable. It should make you uncomfortable. Do you know what else is uncomfortable? Whole units of people with the same diagnosis. Hell, whole hospitals with the same diagnosis, in some cases. This is not normal.

And speaking of normal, I know how badly you want to get "normal" back. I recognize that my face in a respirator is a reminder that things aren't quite normal, despite people's efforts to pretend that they are. Trust me, I want things to be normal too. They just aren't right now, and I will not pretend that they are for you.

Right now, I wear one mask to get from my car to my work locker. Then I put on a different mask to go to the unit. Then I put on my respirator and my eye shield. My hair is covered. We are in gowns and gloves. Negative airflow roars in the background. In every room there is someone whose life is currently not very normal—young, old, strong and healthy, weak and withered. Some are trying to grow new life: moms, dads. Loved ones. This is uncomfortable.

When I come home, I have to strip out of my clothes in my garage. I have a system of cleaning as I get my clothes off to go into my house and see my people. They now remember to stay away from me until I've showered. This, too, is uncomfortable.

I want normal back too. I don't want this to be real either. I don't want to have to tell my tearful four-year-old that we can't go to the YMCA to swim right now. Or my seven-year-old that her art camp was canceled. Both my husband and I work outside the home, and I do not want to make decisions about day care while we are gone. Do I send them to potentially infect their own grandmas, or do I send them to day care at our church and risk the health of ninety-eight other children? Who has to make this fucking awful parenting choice? Who has to think like this? Every time I snuggle up to my children, I think about it. Should I kiss them less? Will that hurt them more? This is not normal. Healthcare workers are dying from this. This, too, is uncomfortable.

I wish I could go back in time and enjoy the shit out of taking them grocery shopping with me, being able to laugh if they licked the cart at Target. I even miss the chaos of trying to get snacks in everyone before dance class. Now, I am soaking up every moment.

I cannot change the fact that this is reality for healthcare workers right now. You want me to zoom out so you can't see my face. Then I'm less real, less scary. Less likely to be your neighbor. My message feels further away. I am sorry. This is also uncomfortable. But you need to hear it. You need to feel uncomfortable, because it is real, and here, and happening.

Over one hundred thousand people have died in a short time. More are dying. There is no vaccine. It is far more contagious than the flu. It has a far longer incubation period, meaning by the time you get sick, you will have already been in contact with many other people. Despite extreme measures, healthcare workers are still getting infected. This is not over. This should be uncomfortable.

And while I'm here babbling and you are probably over me completely, let me say one more thing that's uncomfortable. Gathering in big groups, for any reason, is not medically smart right now. This virus doesn't care that you may have an incredibly valid reason to gather. The protests happening everywhere, while far more important to many than this virus, are still risky. I know that's hard to hear. But it is a fact. This virus doesn't care if you're a big group of douchey spring breakers versus a centuries-in-the-making protest against everything that is awful in this world. This isn't political, this isn't racial, this isn't meant to stir up an emotional argument. This is just an epidemiological fact that everyone should know. And since I am already preaching to try to protect more people, there it is—also uncomfortable.

The year 2020 has been uncomfortable for everyone. ICU nurses are normally well-versed in really uncomfortable conversations. I will not zoom myself out to pretend this isn't real. I will not hide from this to pretend everything is normal. It's emotional. It's heart-wrenching. But it is our reality. So while I'd love to go back to writing funny things about my kids, this also needs to be said: this isn't over.

#covidlife #zoomin

#pandemic #2020

#whileiamatitgetyourflushot

JUNE 2020

Me: Hey, babies, can you maybe think about leaving the bathroom so I can pee in peace?

Kid 1: I am *not* a baby, Mom.

Me: [*. . .*]

Me: And yet you're still here.
#momlife
#noprivacy

JUNE 2020

So we are on Day 100 of quarantine, or maybe a thousand. You know how at some schools they let the kids dress up like old people on the one-hundredth day? I feel like that now, only it is the moms, and we have all aged ten years. Is that a thing? It could be a thing.

21.

Our children have now been home for over a hundred days. Apart from when I am at work, I am home with them. This is, hands down, the most time I will ever spend at home with my kids.

When we shut down in March, I had no idea what this would entail. Before the shutdown, a three-day weekend at home was a "long stretch." I was used to time away, me time, time filled with activities and shuttling around to various obligations. I burned downtime with trips to Target and dinners out. We played, and studied, and ran, and were busy. And then, suddenly, all of that was gone.

Time is now currency. There has been an adjustment period, emotional for all of us. It's been filled with unexplained tears, growing pains, and the squeeze of melding into a new routine where no one has real space, but everyone has plenty of downtime. There are fears to talk about and uncertainty for the future to address. Nobody wants to talk about viruses with a scared, confused four-year-old. But they pick up more than you'd expect. So here I am, discussing the fact that I have no freaking idea what is happening, or what is going to happen, telling him only that we will get through it together.

But we have been growing. I have grown. We have stretched and ached and blossomed into something simple and beautiful. We've gotten better at boredom. We are learning to give each other space while doing more together. We have found beauty in the quiet of a forest, the green engulfing us until we forget about everything else.

We have learned to focus on what we have versus what we don't. I cannot think about vacation, or missed dance classes, or the absolute clusterfuck of the upcoming school year. But I can be the shark chasing them around our backyard. I can draw butterflies in sidewalk chalk outside our little home. I can splash barefoot in a waterfall and search for tadpoles among the reeds. I can take a moment to stop and just hold them. I can breathe in their hair and smell dirt and sunshine.

Never again will I take time for granted. Never again will I not appreciate these minutes. This has been emotional and brutal and awesome. I hope that someday they will look back on this time and remember: their mom chose to help others even when it got scary. Their parents were here, figuring out this new normal together.

I hope they remember to find joy in the simple things. I hope they never forget our summer beneath the trees.

JUNE 2020

Kid 1: Mom, were you as skinny as me when you were my age?

Me: Yeah, I looked like you.

Kid 1: So, when I grow up, I will look like [gestures vaguely at me] all of this?!?

Me: What kind of troll do you think I am?!?

JUNE 2020

My kids said their dinosaurs are getting married. One is currently singing "Kumbaya," and the other is naked, screaming, "Shake your booty!" This seems to be an accurate wedding description. #weddingsinWI

JUNE 2020

Kid 2: Mom, I love you so much because you just have the best face.

Same, little boy. Same.

22.

Before we get back to the awful COVID stuff, let me tell you my favorite work story of 2020. To get the full understanding of this little event, you need me to set the stage. We are now something like a million months into the pandemic. Life is already saturated with change, and everything already feels like it is in overdrive.

Within the last month, the Twin Cities have been engulfed in protests and flames. There are citywide curfews in place, and many of us are unsure of how we will get safely to and from the hospitals. People are lined up on the overpasses waving sheets with spray-painted messages and signs. Chinook helicopters are descending into the city. The national guard has been called out, and the hospital is flanked with armed sentries. I look out the window of the COVID unit and see men in camouflage carrying guns below me. There are bomb threats to the hospitals in the metro, and everyone is on high alert. It is safe to say that our stress level and tolerance for an unexpected "emergency" is low.

Since the COVID unit is entirely negative airflow, it is sealed off at all points from the rest of the hospital. You enter through an anteroom and can hear the rush of air when the door opens. The huge machines inside regulate the airflow within the unit, sucking it outside via giant vents and hoses. What normally is an exit to an outside hallway is now a false wall, sealing us off and maintaining that air suction. Essentially, we are in a giant fishbowl hooked up to a vacuum cleaner.

So when the Exit sign in the hallway outside our unit short-circuits and sets on fire, we are unable to see it. And the downside of our vacuum-powered-super-unit is that the negative airflow will pull smoke inside like we are about to be engulfed by a dang forest fire.

We are all doing nursing cares and charting when smoke starts billowing inside from underneath the sealed doorway exit, like the entrance to hell itself has opened on the unit. Let the ridiculousness commence. The first comical scenario is a bunch of nurses with respirators on attempting to smell smoke. We start smelling something weird, and then notice that a freaking wall of smoke is pouring onto the unit. This unit is filled with enough people on oxygen that my very first thought is that we are now trapped inside a giant-ass bomb.

What occurs next is straight-up, controlled pandemonium. If you want to see a terrific test of Darwinism, set something on fire in a nursing unit, during a pandemic, with riots raging outside. In an instant, there are life decisions being made, and we quickly find ourselves separated into two very distinct camps—the ones who were ready to save all the humans, and the ones that were like "Fuck this. I am outta here." We have nurses deciding where we are going to evacuate a bunch of highly contagious people, and nurses ready to run down the back stairs to freedom.

Suddenly, we are torn between waiting for orders and rolling patients down the hall using computer chairs. We line towels up along the doorjamb and start talking about how many patients we have on ventilators. In an instant, this becomes crisis nursing, and we are having to decide who we are saving first and how much portable oxygen we will possibly need to keep everyone alive.

Thankfully, this is a very short-lived test of humanity. Whatever is burning in the Exit sign is discovered, and an actual crisis is averted. Then, a confused patient accuses us of being pirates because we are wearing funny hats and are all smoking something awful. We all dissolve into relieved laughter, and the moment is added to the list of weird shit that we have lived through this year. Yes, we are COVID pirates. Yo-ho-ho and a bottle of hell no. And we keep going.

JUNE 2020

When there's a fire alarm and smoke coming onto
the COVID ICU, and you learn that the exit sign
set itself on fire . . . Seems fitting for 2020 . . .
#noexit
#itsallburning

JULY 2020

I'm even louder for quite a while after my respirator is off because we're used to yelling to be heard. For those that know me, this is not a good thing.
#alreadyloudAF
#imnotyellingyoureyelling

Progress Note:

Time: 1530, Day 19
Name: Jack, still Jack
VS: T 97.1, esophageal P: 141 BP: 90/43
O2 Sat: 88% on ventilator, 100% and PEEP 16

Patient sats dropping despite prone position and max ventilator support.

MD called. Family to be updated.

I hate this I hate this I hate this I hate this I hate this. God, I am so tired.

23.

Families are one of the most emotional parts of the pandemic for me. At first, I am not going to lie, "no visitors at the hospital" sounds awesome. Empty waiting rooms. Nobody coming up to the nurses' station asking for more water or for their mom to be repositioned. No questions, no recliners, no people taking notes of our every move.

But then, you quickly see how much a patient's morale is affected by family. When someone has COVID and they are in the hospital for weeks on end, the person they were before just disappears. Any light or fight they had just wanes, fading into the breaths and the beeps of the monitors. Nobody they recognize is there to tell them to keep fighting. Nobody is there to remind them of what they're trying to get home to. Nobody is there to keep them focused on recovery. Some try to keep up on their phones, but when you can't breathe, the phone is not very useful. We have done so many videoconferences, but nobody can hear anything over the roar of the machines. You can't hold your mom's hand on a videoconference. It is not the same.

Family cannot understand what their loved ones are going through either, and that makes this extremely hard no matter what is happening. Families worry like crazy and end up calling all the time. We reassure them on the phone, but it is hard to get the point across when they cannot lay eyes on the person they love. And in the other direction, when we need family to know that we have done everything and are still failing, it is hard to convey that because they have not witnessed the effort. They can hear that their dad is on a ventilator, but they don't see all the tubes and lines and medications keeping him alive. They don't see the sores all over his skin from lying upside down. They haven't seen us in action, working day in and day out, trying to save their loved one. They don't understand how much "doing everything" entails, and they cannot fathom what this means for their loved one long term. These conversations deserve to be had in person. And COVID makes that very hard.

Jack is dying. We try everything. Literally everything. He is upside down and right side up for days and days. We draw labs and tweak settings on his ventilator. We give medications to attempt to normalize every vital sign. We dress his wounds and keep them clean. He has a tube in his throat to attempt to help him breathe. He has a tube down to his stomach to feed him. He has a tube in his rectum to catch the poop that we finally got thin enough for him to pass. He has a catheter to drain and measure his urine. He has an arterial line to measure his blood pressure and a venous line to deliver medications. He has special boots on to prevent foot drop. He has soft stickers all over him to cover existing wounds or to prevent new ones. We have bathed him in lavender. We have shaved him. We take his blood sugar often and treat him with insulin. We turn him every two hours like clockwork. We suction his lungs. We clean his mouth. The list goes on and on. And still, we are losing. This is the phone call that a family does not want. If we let you come and visit on the COVID unit, it only means one thing—we are out of straws. Jack gets one visit, for two hours. We try to pick this time wisely. Jack has to pick who comes. He gets one person, two on a rare occasion. So what happens if Jack has three kids? What if he has a baby? What if his wife of forty years has dementia and is too high risk to come in? What if, what if, what if. We call, and it is time to pick.

It is my job to greet you when you come to the COVID unit to have your impending-death visit. I get to come into the hall, welcome you to the unit, and look into your eyes where I see your fear and anguish. I tell you that you get two hours with the person you love more than anyone in this world. I bring you into the anteroom and instruct you to foam your hands. Here, in our back room, we have a few special breathing machines for the purpose of your visit. You take your mask off. You are already tearful. I speak softly, trying to calm you, helping you put the generator around your waist, and hooking the hose into the hood that will go over your head. The flip of a switch brings the rush of airflow, and we put your hood on. I ask you if you are ready. You are not ready in your eyes, but dear God, you always say yes. I swallow the lump in my throat. Let's go in.

Jack looks as good as we can make him. We have straightened up his room and made his sheets look nice. We clean his mouth and put his arms on top of the sheet so you can hold his hand. I put a folding chair by the bed and take down the bed rail. Sometimes we put on some music, although you can't really hear it over the roar of the unit. The sound of your sob, that first catch of your voice, hits me every time. You can't catch tears in your air hood. They just free-fall.

I am so fucking sorry. I am so sorry we couldn't save you, Jack. For a while, we thought you were the one to make it. We should have known. We fought for you, Jack. We wanted you to win. We wanted you to breathe. We wanted you to roll out of here, broken and weak, but whole. We thought you had a chance. I am so, so sorry.

The two hours are up, and the hardest part of all of this is telling you that it is time to leave. The moment of utter despair in your eyes, the breath caught, the tracks of tears on your face is unbearable. But the worst is the look of res-ignation, the steeling of your face and straightening of your shoulders as you nod your acceptance. You turn, to look at your loved one for the last time. You know that this is your last moment.

I cannot look while you take your gear off. I cannot make eye contact with you, or I will lose my shit. So I futz with your machine, cleaning the hood while you gather your belongings. I walk you out and let you go. I see your shoulders slump as you walk away, the physical sign of utter emotional exhaustion. I tell you to drive carefully instead of bawling. I keep it together for you. Sometimes, we hug; sometimes, you thank me. I say of course, like it was noth-ing. Like I let you go in front of me at the grocery store checkout line, or I gave you the last cookie. Not like I am about to help your person die in peace. You are welcome, it was our pleasure, fuck this, I am so sorry. We are all so damn sorry.

Jack is dying today. His breathing tube is removed by the respiratory therapist. Death doesn't take long with these folks. We have medicine to keep them from being in pain, and medicine to keep them from being air hungry. I hold his hand. I smooth his hair. No more breathing, Jack. We are with you, honey. It is okay to let go. Your wife was here, Jack; she loves you. Your brother loves you too. It's okay to go now. You fought so hard, just rest now. Rest, Jack, I am with you. There you go.

Progress Note:

Time: 1603, Day 23
Name: You Know
VS: Don't matter anymore, do they

Time of Death: 1601

Again. Another. Over and over and over. Why, Jack, do I constantly have to tell you good-bye? And yet, I look around the unit and there are more and more of you. Same story. Same passage. Same ending. I need a new story, Jack. You need a better ending. You need a different book. I need a different book. Can I go home yet? Is this shift over? I need to be done.

Oh, wait, I can't. They keep coming.

HUNDREDS OF SCIENTISTS SAY CORONAVIRUS IS AIRBORNE, ASK WHO TO REVISE RECOMMENDATIONS

July 5, 2020, *NY Times*

JOHN LEWIS, GEORGIA CONGRESSMAN AND CIVIL RIGHTS ICON, DIES AT 80

July 17, 2020, *NBC Philadelphia*

MINNESOTA COVID-19 CASES SURPASS 50,000

July 20, 2020, *Minnesota Department of Health*

JULY 2020

Kid 1: So, uh, Mom, let me tell you about a thing that happened this weekend on this rug . . .

Kid 2: I pooped on the rug, Mom!

Me: What?

Kid 1: Yeah, he pooped. But don't worry, I cleaned it up!

Me: Wait—

Kid 2: I pooped, Mom! Right there, see? But we cleaned it, Mom!

Kid 1: [*. . .*]

Me: Wait. What? Why didn't you tell Dad?!

Kid 1: Well, it was my fault because—

Kid 2: It was her fault, Mom!

Kid 1: Well, I wouldn't get off the potty and he had to go—

Kid 2: I pooped a pile right there, Mom!

Kid 1: And Dad would be mad, so we just cleaned it.

Kid 2: Right there, Mom! Right there!

Me: Oh dear Lord! Did you wash your hands?

Kid 1: [*. . .*]

Kid 2: [*. . .*]

Me: Um, thank you. For this information.

Oh my Lord. I've been standing on this rug for days with shit on it.

24.

Oh my gosh, I am so sick of politics. And arguing. And people in general.

Guess what, Democrats and CNN and whatever else is on mainstream media? You're shooting yourselves in the foot. Your reporting is so extreme, and you're pushing your narrative so far that no one believes you anymore. Why is it okay to have a gazillion people gather for a march and not a rally? Both are bad ideas right now.

Guess what, Republicans and Fox News and whatever other source spews hateful crap from the other side of the fence? You cannot ignore a virus. Dear Lord, the president just wore a mask on television for the first time *today*. A little late, yo. A couple of people have died. Remember how much you all shit about Hillary and her emails or whatever? Goodness, you're making that look like child's play.

Libertarians, you're not left out of this rant either. My gosh, I'm annoyed at how much "me me me" is going on in this world right now. You don't want to be told anything by the government, but by God, please care about others enough to wear a freaking mask.

Everyone cares so much about all this junk. Guess what does not care about any of this stuff? This virus. Science. Math. Things without agenda or narrative or conspiracy theories. This virus does not care if you're freaking amazing or if you don't even believe in it. It doesn't care if you're the cutest grandma ever that has been married fifty years and gives homemade Christmas gifts. It doesn't care if you're twenty-five and recently engaged. It doesn't care if you're pregnant with your first baby, and it's a boy, and you're so excited. It doesn't care.

This virus doesn't give a shit that we spent three weeks trying to save you. That we gave you all the magical drugs and plasma and blah blah blah in our arsenal. Nope. You can huff and puff away. Then you're gone, and we lose. Next patient, please. We are all so freaking caught up in the politics that we forget we are fighting an apolitical virus.

How can we fight something that we cannot reason with? We need to band together. We need to fight as a team. Individually, we are losing. Only together can we help the most people. Doing this means you're going to have to think about (gasp) other people. I know this is a foreign concept for many of us lately. Remember Jesus? He wasn't in a political party. He just wanted us to be kind to one another and to help each other. He actually went out of His way, and kindly died to prove His point. Please, stop fighting each other. We're all freaking humans. Please try, for a minute, to let go of the negativity that this society we've created has made, and try to love. Can we please pick love?

And while I am at it, let's go over the damn mask argument again. Why do I keep trying? I have to. I need to. Again, masks are like turn signals. They're a collaborative public safety measure. They help get us from point A to point B more safely, and they prevent stoppage, slowdowns, and accidents. They keep our roads running smoothly because everyone is helping each other.

Yet you don't hear people screaming, "Muh freedoms!" over turn signals! Why? They are the same, aren't they? Nobody is going to arrest you if you don't use one. They help you a little, but mostly they're for other people.

But wouldn't it sound odd to hear:

"Nobody can tell my finger to push that lever!"

"Look at all those people on I-94 living in fear of changing lanes."

"Dang sheep, over there turning left and shit."

Doesn't that sound absurd? Let's take it a step further. Masks, like turn signals, aren't perfect. What if one car on the road is an older model with faulty wiring, or its turn signal is broken? Maybe a couple of vehicles out of the whole group, right? But that doesn't take much away from the whole system, because everyone else is doing their part. If everyone else on the road is using their signals, the few who can't are less likely to impact the whole.

Or let's say Betty is accidently using her turn signal wrong. We've seen it—someone leaves it blinking for miles on the highway before they notice. Does everyone look and yell, "Oh my pearls, that turn signal is not being used right! No one should use these. We are doomed!" No. You give Betty some extra space until she figures her shit out, or maybe you'll go the extra mile and flash your lights at her to try to help her catch on.

But nobody is abandoning turn signals because of a few people that can't use them. Nobody feels like their rights are infringed on by turn signals. Turn signals are just a group safety action that came to pass because cars were getting faster and we needed a change.

Now, I hate masks. Hate them. I hate seeing my kids in them. They break my heart and remind me that the world is not normal right now. But by God, we need to turn together, so we can get off this highway and back onto our nice country roads where we can breathe fresh air. This is a change. But if we do this right, let's pray with everything we have that it doesn't have to be here to stay. And here is a hint—as long as I have to go to work looking like the love child of Darth Vader and the Michelin Man, we're not there.

I am so tired. I am tired of fighting the virus and the public at the same time. Please, Lord, why would we lie to people? Why would I put this ridiculous gear on, and breathe in this gosh-forsaken respirator for twelve-and-a-half-hour shifts if I didn't have to? Why would I strip naked after every shift, painstakingly cleaning everything I touch so I can get my clothes into the wash and myself into the shower before I see my kids? Why would I do that just to lie to people?

We are caregivers, not politicians! We aren't pushing an agenda; we're trying to keep people alive. We aren't withholding treatment. We aren't secret workers trying to take down the presidency. We have bigger things to deal with right now. We're trying to keep businesses running. We're trying to help you.

My actual job is to keep people alive. Anyone who knows me knows that I love this role with every fiber of my being. There is nothing better than being able to put everything I have into saving the life of someone that most likely will never even know my name.

We here in COVID-land are months into this. We are tired. There is no end in sight. I have had only COVID patients since March. We are people, parents, and spouses. We're making the same hard decisions that you are. This sucks. I get it. I hate masks too. I want regular school too. I hate the election too. This is brutal and awful, and I want it to go away too.

There are no good answers. But by God and everything holy, please just try to see that we are on your side. Please see that we are not the enemy. Because I do not have the emotional capacity to prove our moral worth during a pandemic. I don't. I can't. You are breaking me.

I am at work, once again in the rush of the air. Today my patient is pregnant, her swollen abdomen rising and falling with every breath. I am puttering around her room, getting my act together for my shift. Pregnant moms need even more oxygen, higher numbers to protect their unborn child. Her high flow oxygen is as high as it can go, 100 percent and rushing like the air being squeezed out of a balloon. She is talking about her baby, her hands cupping her belly as she speaks to me. Her other little boy smiles at me from a picture on her bedside table.

I am straightening up the room when something makes me look up. I no longer see the rise and fall of her breaths. I look up to the monitor just as it starts to alarm. Her eyes are looking through me, and I scream in my respirator, as loud as I can to call the code.

Time is instantly slowed. The bedside table is shoved aside, the picture falling to the floor as I pull back the sheets and crawl up onto the bed. The first slam of my hands to her chest causes bubbles to start to pour from her mouth.

She is blue gray, and her head is bouncing with every ounce of my effort to bring her back to Earth.

My backup is coming; oh my gosh, where is everyone—seconds seem too long as the other nurses are rushing to put on gowns and join me in this horrific scene. Where is the doctor, I need the doctor, the flat line on the monitor is howling its alarms as we continue to pound. *The baby, the baby, we need to save the baby*, is the only thought racing through my mind. The C-section cart is just outside the room and is pulled, crashing in as another nurse relieves me. Sweat is pouring down my face, and my respirator is sliding against my chin. This is taking too long. The doctors have to get all their gear on, we are running out of time. We need to save the baby.

I pull drawers open, the pulse pounding in my ears. I find a scalpel, and with one more desperate look to the door in hope of seeing somebody, anybody, that can help us, I swallow. The alarms are so loud I cannot think of anything else. The first slice into skin—so many layers, like watching in nursing school—how much farther? Blood is coming now, with each pound of the CPR at the head of the bed. Deeper, deeper, I cut. She can't feel me anyway, deeper and deeper I go, until I find the uterus swollen within the depths of her abdomen. I cut it open and reach into the warmth, feeling for the life within, pulling the tiny body out as . . .

I wake up, sweating. I am looking for blood. It takes me a second to realize that I am not in the hospital. The ringing of the alarms still feels real. In this second, a wave of exhaustion hits me. It was a dream, today. Just a dream. I am losing my fucking mind.

Everyone keeps dying in my dreams now. I try to listen

to my mom talk about the errands she ran today, but instead I am stifling a scream because I let her go last night. I held her hand as we pulled out the breathing tube from her throat, and I watched her skin lose its color. I watched her take her final breath. Oh, wait, she is still talking about going to Trader Joe's. She is still here. She is still alive.

Do you tell your husband that he keeps dying also? Like, "Hey, honey, if you would just stop dying, I would feel a lot better about going to the movies." Because I keep finding myself curled up in the hall of the hospital, waiting as they flip your body over, facedown, to help you breathe. How do you say this to people? How, after seeing this over and over, do you not think that the people you love might be next? How do you rationalize going to the store or going to the movies, if that is the trade-off in my mind? It is freaking hard, and no matter how unlikely or ridiculous it sounds, it is there, just out of reach, ready to remind me when I close my eyes.

I want to be normal for a minute, and not have to worry about these things. We know too much. We have seen too many families who were blindsided by the horror of what this virus can do. It is too real for me now to let it go. Over and over, images burned into my mind. I cannot breathe.

I keep writing. I keep documenting this shift like it is the thread that keeps me tied to the rational world. Maybe my pen to the paper is the only thing keeping me afloat. Documenting this is the only way I can tell the difference between the awful reality we are going through, and the extension of that awful that has seeped into my own mind.

JULY 2020

Is it weird that I get a little mad at any zit that pops up in a non-mask area at this point? Like, get back to your home with the others, you little traitor.
#nurselife
#masklife
#respiratorlife

JULY 2020

Attempted to take the kids to the playground today. It was empty. It seemed safe. Within three minutes, Kid 2 licked a freaking handrail, and this is why we're all screwed.

JULY 2020

You know life is weird when you make Pinterest boards titled things like "Pandemic School Ideas" and "Fun Quarantine Projects."

TRUMP ADMINISTRATION INVESTS $472M MORE IN MODERNA VACCINE CANDIDATE

July 27, 2020, *Politico*

WISCONSIN COVID-19 CASES NOW EXCEED 50,000

July 28, 2020, *Wisconsin Department of Health*

WISCONSIN GOVERNOR ORDERS MASKS STATEWIDE AMID VIRUS SURGE

July 30, 2020, *Associated Press*

WISCONSIN REPUBLICANS "STAND READY" TO KILL GOVERNOR'S MASK REQUIREMENT

August 1, 2020, *Associated Press*

25.

Families. They are one of the reasons I am struggling to function. Their heartbreak is palpable and continuous. They are learning lessons too late. Their salvation is out of reach. Nothing can ease the torment of the marathon that is COVID.

ICU nurses normally have a complicated relationship with family. Family usually means more work, more emotions, more questions. Family comes out to the desk and wants things, wants to know things, wants us to do things. But, as you know now, family looks different in a COVID ICU. Everything is different. Now, you only visit if your family member is dying. A "compassionate exception," we call it.

This means that we are trying to be you, families. And we are definitely not you. These patients are so sick. They are lonely. They've heard the news, and they are so scared. Or they are too sick to speak, lying in silence with only the rise and fall of the ventilator keeping them alive.

We try, families. We hold their hands when they are restless. We try to calm their fears. We cheer for them when they get to walk the unit, oxygen in tow, holding on to us and waving as they take their first shuffling steps outside the room.

But oh, the heartbreak! We hold phones to patients' ears, looking for a spark of recognition when they hear your voices. We FaceTime and try to hold the iPad steady as you say your fervent prayers. We are saying them also, off camera, holding back tears for you. To hear you, your words of encouragement, your love, just makes this more real and more difficult. It reminds us that these people are regular people, with other people that love them. It makes us want to fight harder, but cuts deeper when we lose that fight.

You should know your impact, families. The look on a patient's face when they hear your voice. When we bring in a care package from home and your patient finally agrees to eat. The amazing moment when a patient can be walked to the unit window, and looks down to the street and there, stories below, their children are waiting and waving up at them from the sidewalk. I cannot imagine the unbridled joy of getting to see my mom or dad upright, hands pressed against that window, real and whole. For once, I have tears of joy in this place.

We are here, families. We see the utter beauty in these tiny moments. We are cheering for you, for your loved ones. We are tracking the ones we can send out of the unit, one step closer to you. These moments keep us going when everything we have seen is breaking us down. We are fighting for these beautiful miracles among the flames.

Sometimes Jack lives. This is another part of COVID, and this year, that weighs heavy on my heart. So often with this virus, life and death are the measure of success and failure. But that is not the case, at least within the ICU. There is far more to the story.

Life is a sacred thing within these walls, but it falls on a spectrum. Life is more than a beating heart or a squeeze of a hand. Life, to me, means I can breathe. Life means I can think, and sing, and hug my children. I can go outside under the trees. I can eat ice cream and laugh out loud. Life, to me, is something active and mobile, something I can dive into and enjoy. Life requires participation.

To me, life is fragile, beautiful, and holy. A critical illness puts life into perspective and changes what it means to people. Life is fluid, and sometimes, it is a brutal, heartbreaking thing. Life and death are part of what we do as nurses, but 2020 is pushing the boundaries of both.

Another Jack is awake now. People outside of healthcare do not understand what survival means after two months in intensive care. Jack has been fighting for weeks and weeks now. The staff, myself included, now all know him by name. That is not a good thing. You never want to be the Beyoncé of the ICU, where nurses can refer to you by first name, and everyone knows who you are. And yes, I am using Beyoncé instead of Madonna because then maybe you will think I am younger and forget that I referenced film canisters earlier.

Whatever your one-named celebrity of choice, you do not want to be the Beyoncé or the Madonna or the Cher of the COVID ICU. This means that you have been through hell, and somehow, you've made it through the weeks of lying on your face, the tubes and infections, the delirium and restraints, and the millions and millions of breaths. This time, Jack makes it. He is not counted as a death statistic. But what does this mean for him?

He is a shadow of what he was before this. A broken soul, skin hanging, muscles flaccid, eyes hollow. He most likely has a trach tube in a hole in his neck to help him breathe. He will have a feeding tube placed in his belly to give him nutrients while he tries to continue to heal. He will keep his catheter to pee if he can manage to make any. If not, he will continue to have dialysis for hours every other day. He will not get to go home.

He will go to a long-term-ventilator rehab unit, where he may spend months and months attempting to learn how to move, walk, and breathe again. He will be at risk for more setbacks, more infections. He will find out what his new normal will be. If he is lucky, he may someday return home. But he may have scarring on his lungs forever. He may need dialysis forever. His life, whatever his life was before, will be different forever.

This is what a "win" is for the survivors in intensive care, and that is hard for us also. For as many deaths as haunt my dreams, the survivors are there also. We wonder about them. We swap updates as we learn them. We do not forget them. Seeing Jack live is often just as hard as seeing him die, and again, it pushes us to the limit of what we as nurses can handle. Sometimes Jack breathes. But that does not always make it better.

AUGUST 2020

Buckling child into the back seat.

Kid 2: Mom, I'm going to miss you.

Me: I'm literally going to be in the front seat.

Kid 2: . . . I know.
#quarantinelife
#somuchtogethertime

AUGUST 2020

To celebrate summer, I dyed Kid 1's hair purple. This was at her request, I might add.

I was unprepared. It looks like a purple explosion in our tub. There is actual purple rain. Her neck is purple. Her ears look elfish. She smells like a grape. Her fucking tongue is somehow purple. Everything in the bathroom looks like I murdered a Viking or a Troll doll. Kid 2 is now screaming out of concern for Kid 1's well-being.

This was not my best parenting choice. We'll need a hazmat team just to clean up her face. On the upside, she loves it. And immediately she said, "Dad is gonna hate this."

Truth, child. Truth.

26.

Speaking of Jack and dialysis, do you know how I know there is a God? You probably think this is going to be an amazing miracle story or something about a patient seeing someone from beyond as they die—something super awesome and meaningful.

That would be false. I mean, I have a ton of miracle stories. They are great. But the real reason I know there is a greater power is because of our continuous dialysis machine. For regular folks, this is man's incredibly bad version of a kidney. A CRRT machine's job is to attempt to clear toxins out of your blood when your organs are failing and you are too sick to handle regular dialysis. It runs slowly and gently around the clock, trying to keep you alive when your kidneys have given up.

To start, this machine is huge. It is bigger than I am. If you so much as make eye contact with it, it will launch into a series of piercing alarms that sound like the medical version of a fucking tornado siren. If this happens, the nurse has about twelve nanoseconds to search the tubes running between it and the patient before it starts clotting off and attempting to kill people.

You have to treat this beast with the caution of a freaking bomb. If you don't clamp something correctly, you're going to blast saline or blood everywhere. You have to monitor it hourly to make sure the blood levels in the damn thing don't drop or you'll get air in the circuit. You have to manually empty the man-made pee coming out of the thing, or it has a heart attack and the alarms start again. Each of its filters costs as much as that Amazon guy makes. It is ridiculous.

There is no way a cell, or molecule, or whatever made humans, was sitting around in the primordial sludge and thought, *Dang, we'd better develop into something to clean this guy's blood*, and their buddy cells agreed, thinking, *Yeah that sounds dicey, we'd better make two.*

Humans' best attempt at making a kidney is this terrible, awful, horrible machine. No kidding.

There is a God. And He made kidneys. Truth.

While we are still back in the dawn of humankind, let's also talk about fear. Fear is an emotion, a sense created within us out of necessity. Cavemen with no fear didn't live very long, so those with this sense lived to procreate. Thus, fear was passed down from generation to generation, cultivating us into who we are as a society today.

For the cavemen, a healthy dose of fear is what kept them from eating a poisonous mushroom, or caused them to run to avoid being eaten by a saber-toothed something. Fear was a good thing. Fear kept them alive and strong and able to survive.

Yes, it is terrible that the media today is selling fear. It feeds on your fear and uses fear for political gain. But that doesn't mean that fear is bad, just that it can be manipulated if the fearful are unable to see the difference. Yet people are using "not living in fear" of a virus as an argument to do things that they should be fearful of right now. Maybe not for themselves but at least for others. I'm pretty sure that a caveman hearing about a mysterious illness one cave down the ridge would not go over to check it out and bring it back to his cave family. That cave family wouldn't live.

People are saying that if we are fearful of this virus, we are "hiding in our basement," implying that they, by not wearing a mask, and venturing out all over town, are somehow living their lives better than those who are being cautious. I would argue that the fear I hold is exactly what is needed right now. It isn't holding me back—heck, I volunteered to work in this shit! You could hardly call that *fearful* or *hiding*. But the fear is there. Fear is what reminds me to check my protective gear before entering the unit. Fear helps me make decisions about what my family will eat, or where we will go right now. And that balance between risk and reward is guided by fear.

Fear is what pulses through me when that code-blue button is pushed. It pumps adrenaline into my veins as I pound on a chest, making time slow to seconds as we watch for that flat line to jump, dance, and show life. Fear saves.

Fear is driving the science for this vaccine or treatment. Fear of death. Fear of the economy collapsing. Fear of this awful year becoming a new normal. Fear drives change. Fear drives growth. Fear is needed. Fear is necessary. And you should be proud of that fear.

If fear of this contagious virus, which is taking down hundreds of humans daily, shapes my decisions for the next year, that is a worthwhile emotion, and I will keep it with me until the danger has passed. Because this saber-toothed something is a virus. And I, sure as hell, would rather "hide" awhile to help my people live.

WORLDWIDE CASES OF CORONAVIRUS SURPASS 20 MILLION

August 10, 2020, *The Guardian*

PUTIN APPROVES FIRST COVID-19 VACCINE FOR USE

August 11, 2020, *BBC News*

JOE BIDEN ANNOUNCES SENATOR KAMALA HARRIS AS HIS RUNNING MATE

August 11, 2020, *BBC News*

DEATH TOLL FROM COVID-19 EXCEEDS 1,000 IN WISCONSIN

August 11, 2020, *Wisconsin Department of Health*

27.

Today is my last surge shift on COVID ICU before my hours drop, and I start back to school. This summer was supposed to be my "free summer" with my children; 2020 had other plans.

Every patient, every shift since March, has had the
same diagnosis. The same labs. The same medications. Every single one. We've seen DVTs, heart attacks, pulmonary
embolisms, strokes, and more from this virus. There have
been more "happy hypoxics" than I have ever thought possible. I've had patients who were nineteen years old, and
others who were ninety-one. Some were pregnant. There
were couples, healthcare workers, and families of healthcare workers. People who should have died somehow lived.
People who should have lived often died. All COVID.

Wonderful moments of joy or love. Families pressing
their faces to the windows or waving from the street below.
Care packages so tenderly wrapped. Cheers when people
got to finally go home. Utter relief and elation.

Moments of overwhelming despair. The flat effect of
someone that has been fighting this for weeks and is running out of will. The look on the doctor's face when we've

run out of options and start reaching for answers that aren't there. The knowledge that there will be more.

The teamwork on our unit has been incredible. The preparation that goes into flipping a critically ill patient to their belly, everyone working in symphony to help them breathe. The backward notes written on glass since we couldn't hear each other in the negative airflow. The moving of units, switching of staff, and endless "roll with it" attitudes—this crew has been amazing. To all our other makeshift COVID nurses . . . thanks for making my "very not free" summer one to remember.

P.S. I'll remain on COVID ICU from here on out, but now only half time.

AUGUST 2020

Kid 1: Mom, do you have any scissors?

Me: In the car?

Kid 1: [*. . .*]

Kid 1: Grandma would have some.

Me: [*. . .*]

Me: I see that I've failed you.

AUGUST 2020

Our children discovered that they can talk to each other through their bedroom air vents. Kid 2 just asked me for a screwdriver "so I can climb through the vent to Kid 1's room." It's not even 7:00 a.m. #sendcaffeine

AUGUST 2020

Just spent over a hundred bucks on back-to-school shoes. That pretty much guarantees that school will take place in our living room.
#2020

28.

Gosh, I miss my church. I could use some church right now. There is a lot of talk about church lately, and how opening churches is so important, almost like we should feel guilty for keeping them closed. Maybe it's because I've spent many a sabbath day within the walls of a hospital, but I've accepted that church isn't in a building right now. At work, I feel God everywhere. He is there when we're laying hands on the sickest of His people. He is there when I hold their hand as their soul quietly departs, beyond where I can see. He is with me all the time.

I think of our wonderful congregation. A small mosaic of elderly and disabled folks that put up with my children and their antics within those pews; they're often the only children at the ten-thirty service. I miss them. I miss the singing. I miss the community. But since when is Jesus confined to four walls? As I walk today, I play praise songs in my earbuds, and nature becomes my church. Jesus is here. I have spoken to Him more this year than any. He has heard my tearful prayers. He holds my worries in His heart as His own.

God isn't closed. He's in my children's laughter and the songs of the cicadas. He is within us. And I can spread His love without a church, until I can be there again. If staying out of those walls protects the people I hold dear within them, then so be it. I can go and make disciples. I can spread love and peace. Isn't that what Jesus wants us to do anyway? Church isn't God. And churches won't be closed forever. When they open, I cannot wait to be there. Until then, He's still here. And thank God for that, because I need Him more than ever.

I am not coping. No one is coping. I am fighting the public, trying everything I can to help people understand what we are going through. I don't know how you can keep trying to explain to people, I am told. Um, because I cannot stop. Why? Because Jack is here. They are with me all the time. I cannot stop; I cannot give up. I just can't.

I continue having dreams. In one, I run screaming into a packed bar at home in Wisconsin. I am in my scrubs. I smash a glass on a table, trying to get people to look up. It is silent, and I hear beer dripping off a table onto the floor. But no one can hear me—I am surrounded by plexiglass, a box within the bar. Everyone around me just keeps drinking, eating, talking, while I stand here in the middle. Then I see them, my patients. They are lined up outside the bar, faces in the window. They are watching me, disappointed. Some are shaking their heads. *This is not going to work*, they think. *They will think you are crazy, and nobody will listen if they think you are crazy*. I fall to my knees in this box, in the bar, and cry hollow, howling tears. Jack watches. I cannot lose my shit. I am letting them down.

Another dream . . . I am on a cliff, with churning water far below me. Other healthcare workers are there, all in our hospital gear. We are holding hands, backs to the open air behind us. We are trying to hold back an enormous crowd, all trying to walk off the cliff. The mass of humans goes back as far as I can see, and they are pushing us to the edge. Everyone is yelling.

My toes are gripping the ledge, I hear the scrape of my shoes as I hold on as tight as I can. People are mad at us; they want to keep going forward. They don't understand that they will fall. People keep breaking through our chain and dropping to the water below. Over and over, I hear the splashes above the roar of the crowd. I cannot look down. We have tears running down our faces, but we can't look down at the bodies floating, because more and more keep pushing forward. The nurse beside me slips and goes over. I hear her shriek, and I let go before I get pulled down with her. There is no time to watch her fall. I lock eyes with the next nurse over, and we reach for each other. I see the bodies floating below us and feel the crowd push harder against me. We link hands and keep going.

I have never had to fight this hard for something that people did not understand. I know I am not alone in this. The fight against the public is one of the hardest parts of all of this, and it is why so many of us have suffered alone. We do not have time to process what we are going through. We do not have time to feel anything. We just need to hold on and keep pushing forward.

I am still writing. I write to get out my emotions. I attempt to get people to understand the importance of the public health measures. I have emailed anyone who I think might listen. To me, science is objective. Epidemiology is objective. This virus does not care who you voted for. This virus has been made political, and the aftermath is that people have no trust in any of it. People think we are lying, and that is what hurts most of all. We, the healthcare workers, are being seen as manipulative. Like we don't have enough to deal with, like we are lying just to pick fights with people. As though we are the kind of people who get joy in controlling the behaviors of others. I've even heard it said that we are withholding some kind of secret treatment in order to fuel a political fire . . .

Life has gotten really ugly. It is hard to be the caregiver when we cannot even get people to think about their neighbors. It is hard to go to work and hold the hands of the dying, and then be told that we are exaggerating things to create fear. This kind of stuff messes with my head. It makes me doubt who I am. It makes me question if this job is worth doing. I cannot wrap my head around the two realities we are living in.

Jack is with me all the time at this point. He reminds me of what is important. He reminds me why I am fighting to get people to understand. The news is so hateful and so divided. People have so many opinions. I am so sick of people. Politics is turning this virus into something even uglier than it is, which is saying a lot when you have seen what we on the inside have seen. Politics is making us forget about humanity. It is making us selfish. It is making me slowly lose my mind.

I am struggling. There is fear in everything now. I know this is irrational, but it is hard to separate what's rational from reality when all I see is the awful. I do not want to go anywhere. I am scared any time my child coughs. I do not like going inside any building. It gets so bad that I can be watching an old movie, and I start thinking that there are too many people in the wedding scene. When will I be able to watch a wedding without thinking of a virus?

I recognize that I am not coping well, but that does not really fix it. Nobody is coping right now, so who can help me? We are all in the same boat. The same, sinking boat. I have to stay the course, one day at a time. I go on an anniversary trip with my husband. A road trip, of course; I could never handle a plane right now.

We go to a casino. They have precautions in place. They take my temperature. People are in masks. I am in a mask. It does not matter. I am filled with panic, guilt, and anger. I am sweating. I cannot breathe without thinking of everyone else's air. When am I going to be able to go anywhere without thinking about breathing in everyone else's air? I feel guilty for even being in the building. I want a sign around my neck saying that I should not be here. I am angry at everyone that did choose to be here. I am watching people, trying to decide who has COVID. Who would live, who would not? The bells and whistles remind me of the beeps of the monitors. The lights flashing are the lights of the ventilators. I am losing my mind. I am not okay. Jack is here. He disapproves. I am not okay. Please, God, help me. Please help me.

I look at my husband, who is unaware that I am losing my mind. That I want him to help keep me sane. What a horrible thing to ask of someone. That is not fair. I am heartbroken for a moment, for letting him bring me here. For not understanding how not-okay I am. Fuck. I look like I keep it together. Why can I not be a good nurse, a good wife, and a good mother at the same time? Why is my love for people making me bad at this? Why do I care so dang much? Why is this pandemic making everything harder? I feel terrible for him. It is not his fault. It is nobody's fault. We are all doing our best. Nobody really understands. How was my day? Do you really want to know? Nobody wants to know now. Nobody really gets it. We are alone in this fight. It isn't real to anyone else.

I cannot handle this. I cannot handle regular people right now. I cannot handle politics. I cannot handle the hate, anger, and division. Yet I want nothing more than to be in this, to be the helper. Now, the only time I feel okay is in that roaring unit, laying hands on the dying. It is the only time I can think straight, the only time that everything feels real. The only time I can ignore the outside world. God, this is taking a toll. Please keep me strong; I need to be stronger than this. One day at a time. One breath at a time. Damnit, just breathe.

JOE BIDEN OFFICIALLY BECOMES THE DEMOCRATIC PARTY'S NOMINEE

August 19, 2020, *The Washington Post*

GLOBAL DEATH TOLL FROM VIRUS SURPASSES 800,000

August 22, 2020, *NY Times*

RESEARCHERS FIND THE FIRST US CASE OF COVID-19 REINFECTION

August 28, 2020, *The Hill*

TRUMP ADMINISTRATION ANNOUNCES VACCINATION DISTRIBUTION PLAN

September 16, 2020, *Politico*

SEPTEMBER 2020

Hey, Jesus, hey, Moses,
Could you look down below us
folks here could use your kind.
The sea isn't just red
There's blue too instead
But we're drowning—
don't leave us behind.
The sea's just as salty
And choppy and faulty
I promise it will make you just frown.
It's political crazy
And looking hazy,
Never mind, just let us all drown.

RUTH BADER GINSBURG DIES: SUPREME COURT JUSTICE WAS 87

September 18, 2020, *Deadline*

COVID-19 CASES IN WISCONSIN HIT 100,000

September 20, 2020,
Wisconsin Department of Health

COVID-19 FACT-FINDING LEADS TO THREATS AGAINST HEALTH WORKERS IN MINNESOTA

September 25, 2020, *MPR News*

MINNESOTA SURPASSES THE 100,000 MARK IN COVID-19 CASES

September 27, 2020,
Minnesota Department of Health

PRESIDENT TRUMP AND FIRST LADY MELANIA TRUMP ARE POSITIVE FOR COVID-19 AND TRUMP IS HOSPITALIZED AT WALTER REED MEDICAL CENTER FOR TREATMENT

October 2, 2020, *AJMC*

29.

At my very first nursing job, the unit I worked on had paired rooms. It was a postsurgical unit, and we purposely avoided putting patients with the same surgery in the same room. They would often compare notes, and if one had complications, it would freak out their neighbor, leading them to think that they could be next.

Today, on our COVID ICU, as I watch the rare occurrence of a patient who is actually able to walk, I cannot fathom how difficult it must be for them to see a whole unit with his same diagnosis. How terrifying it would be to shuffle by room after room of people on ventilators, people prone onto their bellies, people confused and pulling off their CPAPs, knowing that all of them could be them. Seeing that they are clearly the only one here that can walk more than a few feet, if that. They are one of the few that are even coherent. How would that feel? To know that as you struggle to catch your breath, you are the best of the worst. I cannot imagine that fear.

30.

At the end of life, we're all the same. When you are in that bed, dwarfed by tubes and wires, I don't know who you are or what you believe in. I don't know if you're nice to your neighbors or a hateful SOB. And you know what? I don't care.

I don't care what you look like. I've seen people with gang tattoos asking for their mothers, and cute little grandmas with dragon tattoos where you shouldn't find dragons. I've seen pieces of couch removed from where a person actually grew into it. There were maggots and lice, and I don't care; you're all the same to me. I'll braid your hair and scrape the dry skin off your heels and wipe the crust from your eyes with a warm washcloth all the same.

I don't care who you voted for. When you're dying, no one talks politics. I don't know your stance on abortion or the Supreme Court or the magical recovery of the president. I don't know if you wore a mask, or you went out barhopping during a pandemic. I only hear the beeps of the machines, and the soft rise and fall of the ventilator as I keep you alive. Because when death comes, you're all the same.

When it's your time, I will give you medicine to take away your pain. I will keep you from gurgling. I will call for a priest or FaceTime your family. If you've taken your last breath, I will lie to your daughter overseas so that she believes the last words she is telling you over the phone are being heard. They are—by me. And I'll hear them with tears in my eyes because you were loved, and that's all that matters.

Nurses don't care because it doesn't matter. When you reach me, I'll treat you well no matter who you are. I will try my best to save you or give you peace when you need to let go. In this world right now, there's so much hate, stress, and division. Please remember that at the end of this life, we are all the same. We are all humans, and we need love.

OCTOBER 2020

Kid 1 keeps asking for expensive toys for Christmas and then says, "Good thing you don't have to pay for these!" since Santa is on the job. She is playing me, and I am losing.

OCTOBER 2020

Kid 1: Mom, if you ever find a body to bring home, it would be cool to dissec—

Me: Find . . . a body? Like a human? Girl, I cannot just—

Kid 1: Okay, fine. An animal, then.

#dissection
#medicalchildgoodlord
#wheredoesmommyjustfindbodies

U.S. RECORDS 100,000 CASES IN A DAY FOR THE FIRST TIME

October 22, 2020, *NY Times*

"INFODEMIC" COMPLICATES WISCONSIN'S PUBLIC HEALTH FIGHT AGAINST CORONAVIRUS

November 6, 2020, *Wisconsin Watch*

MISREPRESENTATIONS OF COVID-19 DATA ARE SPREADING ON SOCIAL MEDIA, MAKING IT HARDER TO SLOW THE PANDEMIC

November 6, 2020, *MPR News*

COVID-19 DEATH TOLL IN MINNESOTA PASSES 3,000

November 18, 2020, *Minnesota Department of Health*

31.

We are nine months in. That means nine months of ridiculous pictures. Nine months of the same diagnosis. Nine months of trying to get people to understand.

So much oxygen. So many breaths: in, out, in, out. Way too shallow, way too fast. Lungs that you can feel as well as hear. We're numb to the oxygen saturation alarms now. They beep all the time; 70s to go to the bathroom, 60s means they took their oxygen off to blow their nose. Oh, look, they're getting blue. Keep breathing, just keep breathing. Breathe. Please breathe.

Speaking of breathing, we are used to our respirators now. My nose is officially made out of whatever Lance Armstrong's crotch is made of. My chin will never be clear again. And I'm used to the deep breaths through the filters and the hoarse voice after yelling to be heard for hours on end. I'm used to stripping naked in my freezing garage at the end of the shift. My kids are used to not coming near me until I've showered. We've adapted to this new, insane normal.

I've watched people die upside down now. Sedated, paralyzed, their faces swollen and unrecognizable. Some with giant clots. Some with cardiac arrhythmias. Some literally burn up. Many just drown. We hold their hands. We tell them they aren't alone. We tell them it's okay to stop fighting. We call their families and tell them we were there. Tell them we did our best to stand in. Tell them they're at peace. We were there.

Regular nasal cannula oxygen runs at two, four, and maybe six liters. These folks are using forty or fifty liters for days and days. Many can't eat because there's so much oxygen blasting in them that they'll choke. If their oxygen tubing falls off, you've got seconds until they're struggling to recover. It's like a freaking garden hose of oxygen. I'm hosing these people down, and they're not growing. I'm a shitty gardener. Ask my mom.

We lost our resource nurse long ago. Then went our nurses' aide. We are running on double shifts, caffeine, and swear words. We are running on solidarity. We need each other. We run on the idea that we just have to keep going. To survive. To push ahead, one day at a time, until the storm passes and we can see some kind of reprieve.

I write about this for me. It's therapy for me. Because maybe writing it down makes it more tangible, since this shit feels surreal. Maybe someday I can look back on my words, soak all of this in, and remember; remember what it was like to fight a virus people didn't even believe in. To watch hospitals fill up with patients. To build a unit that sounds like a hurricane. To know without a doubt that this is what I was made for. Someday I'll look back. Someday I'll grieve.

For now, they keep coming.

WISCONSIN HOSPITAL LEADER URGES EVERS, REPUBLICANS TO UNITE

November 19, 2020, The Pioneer Press

ILLNESS, STRESS FILL A COVID-19 UNIT AS WISCONSIN LEADERS STALEMATE

November 20, 2020, MPR News

HEALTH CARE WORKERS SCRAMBLED TO TREAT PATIENTS ON A DAY WHEN 92 WISCONSIN LIVES WERE REPORTED LOST. OUTSIDE OF THE HOSPITAL, POLITICIANS POSTURED

November 20, 2020, MPR News

COVID-19 DEATH TOLL IN WISCONSIN HIT 3,000

November 21, 2020,
Wisconsin Department Of Health

CONFIRMED COVID-19 CASES WORLDWIDE EXCEED 60 MILLION

November 26, 2020, CDC

NOVEMBER 2020

I am cooking dinner. Kid 1 comes into the kitchen wearing a mask and holds up a sign: "Mom's Cooking Stinks. This Is Why I Am Wearing a Mask."
#thisiscrap
#momlife

NOVEMBER 2020

On a walk downtown:

Kid 1: Mom, what does the MH on that sign mean?

Me: Uhhh, I think it means "manhole" since there's a manhole cover below it.

Kid 1: MANhole! What about WOMANhole?

Me: Uh, YEAH!!!

Kid 1: I'll cover the *M* up. Now it just says HOLE.

#manholeequality

NOVEMBER 2020

Kid 2: Mom, why aren't you wearing your other robe?

Me: Meh, that one is a little small.

Kid 2: [*. . .*]

Kid 2: Is it because of your butt?

WISCONSIN REPUBLICANS DIFFER ON VIRUS RESPONSE

December 1, 2020, *The Pioneer Press*

WEST VIRGINIA IS THE 50TH STATE TO CERTIFY THE ELECTION RESULTS JOE BIDEN IS THE NEXT PRESIDENT OF THE UNITED STATES

December 9, 2020, *CNN*

PFIZER VACCINE IS APPROVED BY THE FDA

December 10, 2020, *FDA*

COVID-19 DEATHS IN WISCONSIN EXCEED 4,000

December 12, 2020,
Wisconsin Department of Health

FIRST COVID-19 VACCINE GIVEN TO U.S. PUBLIC: A NURSE IN NEW YORK WAS AMONG THE FIRST TO RECEIVE THE SHOT MONDAY MORNING

December 14, 2020, *Wall Street Journal*

FIRST DOSES OF COVID-19 VACCINE LAND IN MINNESOTA

December 14, 2020, *MPR News*

FDA APPROVES MODERNA COVID-19 VACCINE

December 18, 2020, *FDA*

MINNESOTA COVID-19 DEATH TOLL SURPASSES 5,000

December 24, 2020, *Minnesota Department of Health*

32.

There is nothing compared to an ICU during the holidays. Normally, I love my job most at this time of year. There is something special about driving in the deep cold when there are few cars on the road and most buildings are dark. The hospital is ablaze with light, never sleeping, never empty. This year is even more poignant, as our patients will be spending the holidays alone.

Today will be the clearing-out day: the last-ditch effort by doctors to get every patient home who is able to go. It's the last chance to discharge people back to their families for the holiday. Sometimes the doctors' efforts win, and the majority clear out, leaving staff in the eerie quiet to care for only those who cannot leave. There is a beauty in caring for the sickest of the sick on days where everyone else is home celebrating. There is a quiet sadness in the air, and the patients who realize the day have a certain resolve. I can feel it in the halls and see it in the polite smiles.

I love these moments because they give us all a connection, a silent bit of humanity, an extra moment to care and feel. Nursing doesn't have to be a religious experience, but in the moments of dark and calm where I lay a warm blanket on the dying when the rest of the world is tucked home celebrating . . . I feel God. He is here. You can call Him whatever you want, celebrate Him in any way you want, but He is in the very breath of everything we do. And that is why I love working these days, because sometimes I feel like it's my best way to celebrate Him.

This year, however, brings little celebrating within these walls. Christmas and the weeks following are the worst of the pandemic for us in the Twin Cities. The aftermath of Thanksgiving gatherings brought a wave of patients to the hospital. The holidays are spent in the rush of oxygen. We are used to being at an overflowing capacity at this point, but the severity hits me one morning after breakfast on the unit.

Normally, our COVID unit gets meal trays at certain times during the day, and we return them in a cart to be washed. They collect this cart three times daily to reduce the chance for infecting others. This morning, one of the nutrition staff came to collect the cart, and I had no trays to give him.

"I am here to pick up your dirty trays," he says. I pause, thinking that I missed the mealtime. Then it sinks in—not one human on the unit can eat today. Not one person can breathe enough to eat.

"There are no trays," I say. He thinks I don't understand.

"I am here for your dirty trays," he repeats.

"I know," I say. "There are no trays this morning. No one can eat."

"What do you mean, no one can eat?" He repeats my statement as a question and then his eyes shift, and he understands. "Oh, God, I am so sorry," he says.

"Yes, me too." Me fucking too. He looks at me as he exits the anteroom to the rest of the hospital. As I close the door for him, I hear him say thank you. Three times that day, I had the same conversation, and each time it was a punch in the gut. Yes, I have a full unit. No, not one can eat today. Yes, I am sorry too. Breathing comes first. Breathing wins. Nobody can breathe.

So much oxygen, so many ventilators. Silence, on the unit. Nobody eats. No one can use a call light. Nobody needs to get up to the bathroom anymore. No one can talk to family on the phone. Just silence and air.

We learn that there is limited amount of air pressure possible within the building. What does this mean? This means that the actual building has a maximum level of oomph it can provide, and we are close to hitting that limit. The *actual building* cannot handle any more ventilators after that point. I mean, I have worried about staff burnout and worried about running out of equipment, but now we have to worry about building burnout? Oh, 2020, you keep bringing new worries.

I went into this year wide-eyed and full of hope. Instead, this year has tested every ounce of my patience, sanity, and soul. In the chaos, I am learning to slow down. Against my will, I am attempting to take things one day at a time, which is definitely not my natural setting. There was utter beauty in spending days and days with my children in the green of the forest, and joy in watching them blossom within the little world we created at home. Thank God for the simple blessings.

I learned to appreciate my coworkers and my village more than ever. The strength that people have put into our profession this year is unlike anything I've ever seen. I'm so freaking proud of us. 2020, you were a hurricane. Praying for the storm to pass in 2021. Until then, one day at a time. Happy New Year to all.

DECEMBER 2020

Kid 2 thinks the song goes:

> "We wish you a Merry Christmas and a
> Happy New Weird."

And the way this year has gone, he's not wrong.

DECEMBER 2020

Kid 1: Mom, I learned how much I love Kid 2 this
year, because we spent so much time together. I
mean, he still annoys me sometimes, but still . . .
My heart.
#silverlinings

DECEMBER 2020

New Year's Eve: I would like it on the record
that I made it up the longest. To 9.52 p.m.
#byeeeee2020

33.

Documenting this is cathartic for me. Admitting weakness is not my strong suit. I take pride in keeping my shit together. I think nurses as a whole like to be able to manage no matter what is happening during their shift. And moms in general are expected to keep every ball in the air and make it look effortless. We are the ones in charge of the details—the ones who know when the next dentist appointment is and what size shoes their youngest is in now. We keep track of conference dates and ballet recitals and the ever-popular "What's for dinner?" We are the teeth brushers, the photo album makers, the sandcastle builders. We are supposed to be the glue that keeps the family together.

Healthcare moms are next level. We are trained to be immaculate, detail-oriented, and comforting, while running on caffeine and beast mode. We have compartmentalizing down to an art form. I can normally leave an epic code and go home without blinking an eye. I can thump out CPR, yell out medications—the cacophony of sounds is deafening in the silence of my drive home. Then I walk in the front door, listen to the happy squeals of my children, and let it all go.

Up until this year, my job has made regular life better. Life is brighter, sharper focused, when you are the story keepers of illness and death. My stories keep me humble. They remind me that I am human, and how this walk on Earth is fleeting and precious. My stories normally help me fully soak up my existence and squeeze every ounce of joy and love and awe I can get out of it. Nursing allows me to understand how lucky I am, and my love for this profession can fuel every other aspect of this awesome life. Nursing is part of who I am, and that bleeds into everything.

But now, nursing is harder than ever. Instead of making me appreciate humanity, it makes me feel angry, hopeless, and alone. Instead of making me feel lucky and strong, I feel anxious and fragile. The stories in my head weigh heavily; they are needing to be told.

So I am here, writing them down. Because maybe then I can let them go. I am setting them free. Maybe if you read about them, they will leave me. They will get the honor they deserve. Telling the story of this year helps keep them alive. It makes their fight real and worth the toll it is taking on us.

We are here in the woods, watching the trees.

We know of the noises they made; we witnessed their fall. Theirs was the roar of air, the sound of a breath. So many breaths, so many trees. A forest of trees has all fallen silent. We heard you. We remember you. These words are for you, so we remember the beauty of your fight.

I am documenting this shift for every nurse that is feeling alone this year. For every respiratory therapist that is torn between anger and anguish. For every mom doing her fucking best when everything is uncertain. For every person in the public for whom this pandemic feels surreal.

These words are for you, to honor one of the hardest years of our lives.

I am documenting this to show that this year was not a loss, that I am learning from this experience, and will be a better human for it. I am writing this so that someday I can look back and know that each day was a choice, and the sum of those choices made up a life worth living. I am proud of my choice to volunteer. I am proud that I was witness to Jack and his many lives. This is for the hundreds of thousands of lives lost: you have left an imprint on healthcare forever.

What am I learning? I am learning to take each day as it comes. I started off 2020 with a flowery planner filled with fluffy goals like "lose five pounds" and fun vacation ideas. These long term plans disappeared, and I was left feeling lost and adrift without them. It has been a huge shift to take each day for itself and let God figure out the rest. I am learning to appreciate the simple beauty in life when everything slows down enough to see it. My daughter learned how to ride a two-wheeled bike this year. My son gave up his pacifiers and graduated from his crib to a big-boy bed. They learned how to play together, with sticks and mud and whatever can be found in the forest beneath the green of the trees.

I now find God everywhere, from the rush of a waterfall to the peace of a final breath. He keeps me sane when the noise of the world gets to be too much. He is love, and love matters. Love is greater than politics. Love is stronger than hate. Love heals. Love is why, when faced with an unknown contagion, legions of healthcare workers marched into battle. Love is why we fight so hard for every Jack. Love is why he hangs on so long. Love is why he knows it is okay to let go. Love is why we are here. If I know anything at all, it is that love wins. Love keeps me going, even when I have nothing left to give. Love is what this world needs more of. Love endures.

My vaccine is on the horizon, and I can't stop crying. I cry for my patients, for every Jack. We could not save them, and yet this shot I am getting may keep others from his same fate. I cry, thinking that maybe someday, I will be able to go to work and never meet another Jack, that this shift could finally be over, and he will finally be just another story to keep.

When my vaccine day arrives, I feel all the feels. Utter, soul-exhausting relief. You really don't think of fear when you sign up for this. You don't think about it when you're in the thick of the beeping machines and roar of the airflow. You don't think about fear when you're the one watching the numbers, the breaths, laying hands on the ones who are suffering . . . but it's there. It is there when I leave my shift and start thinking about everything I am touching before I go into the house. Fear is in the first hug from my children after my shower. Fear has been here, lurking in quiet undertones, ever since I said yes.

I feel relief. The relief is real and probably not fully understandable to anyone except those of us on the front lines. Watching nothing but the awful for months straight skews your fear, twisting it inside you—even if you know you are likely to be fine. It is a kind of mental torture. The relief is tangible. The relief is freeing. Even now I have not fully grasped what this relief means for me.

I feel heartbreak and guilt knowing that every death in the ten-plus months of this may have been prevented by the very shot I am getting at this moment. That every strangled last breath, every sobbing family member, every catch in my throat trying to keep it together might have been prevented if this tiny miracle had existed before it was needed. Impossible, but I feel it just the same.

I wanted to bring three hundred thousand of something to this appointment, to somehow represent the souls that this moment is honoring, but the number is so great that I'd be honoring them with something lame like paper clips, and let's be honest, that doesn't do anybody justice. I'll settle for words. This is for all of you.

And I feel joy. That this is the beginning of everything we've fought for. This is a tiny light in what has been the darkest of years. This is a chance for a future that looks better than today. This is for when we can all hug again, for when we can have a birthday party or a wedding and see something besides risk versus benefit. This is for the moment when my kid can lick a grocery cart without giving me a stroke. You know, the important shit.

Utter, awesome joy. This moment is one of science, sweat, prayers, and swear words.

For the first time in a very long time, this feels like hope.

WISCONSIN COVID-19 DEATH TOLL EXCEEDS 5,000

January 6, 2021, *Wisconsin Department of Health*

WISCONSIN CORONAVIRUS CASES HIT 500,000

January 8, 2021, *Wisconsin Department of Health*

"THIS IS NOT A GAME": GLOBAL VIRUS DEATH TOLL HITS 2 MILLION

January 15, 2021, *AP News*

JOE BIDEN INAUGURATED THE 46TH PRESIDENT OF THE UNITED STATES

January 20, 2021, *SENATE.GOV*

COVID-19 DEATHS IN MINNESOTA EXCEED 6,000

January 21, 2020, *Minnesota Department of Health*

JANUARY 2021

My house is officially clean. My next semester can start now. If nobody could eat, play, or poop for the next four months, that would be great. #gradschoolmomlife

JANUARY 2021

Kid 1 just made a pros-and-cons list regarding the flavor of her birthday cake. She's mine.
#TypeA
#listsarelife

JANUARY 2021

Both of our children said that they liked what
I made for dinner. If anyone knows the where-
abouts of my *actual children*, let me know.
These two are clearly imposters.

JANUARY 2021

Kid 2: How *cold* is it in this house?!

Me: You *could* put on pants.

Kid 2: Mooooooommmmm . . .

JANUARY 2021

Kid 2: Would you be a dear and put this in the garbage?

Me: [*. . .*]

Me: [*. . .*]

Me: How old *are* you?!

JANUARY 2021

I just watched the first episode of *Bridgerton* . . .
Whelp, grad school, we had a good run.
#shouldbestudying
#nextepisodeplease

Progress Note:

Time: 1437, Day 1
Name: Jonathan Doe
DOB: 07/03/1953, age 67
VS: T 102.4, oral P 122 BP 97/53, left arm
O2 Sat 77% on room air, improved to 92% on 5L
nasal cannula

Patient presents to the ED this afternoon with complaints of shortness of breath, fever, cough. Symptoms started 8 days ago. COVID swab pending.

Dear Lord, they keep coming. Here we go again . . .

WISCONSIN REPUBLICANS PROPOSE GETTING RID OF MASK MANDATE

January 22, 2021, *The Pioneer Press*

WISCONSIN GOVERNOR ISSUES NEW MASK MANDATE AFTER GOP REPEAL

February 4, 2021, *Associated Press*

34.

Almost a year in, and we are still fighting this virus. Almost a year in, and I am still having the mask discussion. The fact that this is still a debate is heartbreaking and mind-blowing, and it is why I need therapy. That a pandemic can bring out selfishness and ugliness instead of community and love is horrifying. That Darwin's Survival of the Fittest is winning over What Would Jesus Do, to me, represents everything that is wrong in this world.

This will be one of my biggest takeaways from this whole experience—that we as human beings need to care for each other, and that the health of the whole is more important to me than convenience for the few. To me, that concept is what separates us from the animals. Compassion. Kindness. Love. Man, we could use some more of that around here.

Writing all of this over the last year has reminded me of what is special about my story: that it isn't special, really. That healthcare is a team sport, and that a global pandemic means that my story has been lived out in thousands of different ways all over the world. That there are people living this shift with me, and that they might recognize pieces of themselves and their experience in these words. That I have not been alone in this. And that makes this documentation all the more important, because it isn't just for me. I am writing this for so many of us who struggled this past year. We were trying to balance love and sanity. We were unable to express what they were going through. We were afraid that if we admitted we were falling apart, the admission alone may be the breaking point, and we could not afford to be broken at this time. This may take a really long time to heal from, and together, our storytelling may help that healing begin. Nurse stories are necessary. Nurse stories can help us slowly find our way back to humanity.

FEBRUARY 2021

Kid 1: Mom, has anyone in our family ever won the Nobel Peace Prize?

Me: [*snort*] . . . Um, no, honey . . . but *you* should!

Kid 1: Yeah, I am not peaceful enough for that . . .

Kid 1: [*. . .*]

Me: [*. . .*]

Kid 1: Is there a Nobel Violence Prize?

FEBRUARY 2021

Kid 2 just took a tiny floatie out of the bath toys,
put it behind his neck, leaned back into the water,
and said, "Ahhhhhhh, just livin' the life."
Who is this child?!

Healthcare workers love humanity.

I freaking *love* humans. I could not do my job if I didn't. Human interaction is what keeps me on my toes and makes the work I do interesting. No two humans are alike, and nurses collect these interactions like trading cards. We have a million stories collected, and someday we will look back on this year and it will be just another tale to tell, another chapter in a career filled with human stories.

People's stories are why my job is worth doing. Every day is unique, and I get to go home knowing that I helped someone. I think that was why 2020 has been so difficult, because for the first time in my life, I have felt separated from humanity. It feels like a breakup of sorts—and it has been, in many ways. I am the high school girl, in love with someone who does not feel the same way. Even if you love people, you cannot make their choices for them. No matter how hard you try, you cannot control others' behavior, even when you believe you know what is best for them. It stings. It feels like a betrayal, to care so much for people when they do not care about themselves or each other. I have had to care a little less—to let it go, to keep from losing my mind. And that breaks a nurse's heart.

Today the United States surpassed half a million deaths from COVID-19. Every death I have witnessed in the last year was from this virus. By the time you are reading this, the pandemic may be over. By the time you are reading this, there could be another two hundred thousand dead. I do not know what the future will bring. I have quit looking ahead. I only can think of today, and remember to breathe.

I hope that by getting this out, I can begin to heal from this year. I hope that by reading this, you can too. Maybe talking about it will help it fade. I honestly do not know when I will feel normal again. Even vaccinated, I struggle with being inside. I have yet to truly wander around Target or go into a clothing store. I took my daughter to get our toes painted for the first time in a year, and it was still hard. I still think of everyone's breaths. I still cannot relax. Jack is still with me. He is not a story yet.

There is a soul exhaustion I keep feeling. The kind where you think you need a vacation, or time away, but there is not enough time to fix this. You cannot self-care this feeling away. I think it needs to be lived, for more time to pass, for it to slowly disappear, and for stability to return. I want to be able to make plans again and not feel like they are subject to change. I want to be able to go to the grocery store with my kids. I want to go on a date with my husband and be able to forget about Jack. I want to be able to breathe without hearing Jack breathe. I want to document this and go home. I want to feel normal again.

So, Jack, this is the end of my shift. I am giving your care over to the next nurse. I need to be able to drive home without you. I will not forget you, the many versions of you. I will not forget your fight, the horrifying beauty in your numbers. I will never forget the year of the same diagnosis. I will never forget the impact you had on my heart, my family, and this amazing profession. I know now that I love what I do more than I love myself. I know I will do this work even when this world is breaking me, and that nurses are capable of amazing things. You all deserve these words, this story, so that you can live forever in these pages. Love means more than hate. Being a mother is more fulfilling than I ever appreciated. And when life gets hard, I need to give it over to God. Above all else, I know now that everybody just needs to breathe.

If you didn't document it, it didn't happen.

But this did happen, so here it is I am done now; I need to head home. Back to the My Little Ponies, to nature, and to after-shower hugs. Back to just being Mom, back to being a wife, back to just being me.

Jack, I hope I did you justice in this shift. I truly gave it my all.

I will end this the way we end all nursing notes, because it fits—*will continue to monitor.*

Good-bye, Jack. Good-bye, all of you.
Thank you for letting me care for you.
It was the honor of a lifetime.

AFTERWORD

One week after I submitted this book to my editor, in March of 2021, the COVID ICU unit was dismantled. As quickly as it was built, it was taken down. Gone, practically overnight. Gone was the false wall that boasted red warning signs telling people to beware. Gone were the pictures of the PPE required to enter. The entrance to the anteroom—our window into the world of roaring air and the home of Jack—that was gone too. All that remains are the remnants of the negative airflow hoses, standing silent now, like the skeletons of buildings left after a war. One full year within those walls, one full year of Jack and his countless breaths, has dissolved into nothing.

We, the COVID volunteers, have been dispersed back into the general ICU population without missing a beat, as if the entirety of 2020 had never happened. But we know. I see it in my former colleagues, a quiet unsettling. It is what I imagine soldiers feel after coming home. We are expected to return to normal. The world is returning to normal. But we are dragging emotionally behind, blinking in the sunshine like bears after winter. There are still a few COVID patients, but they are low enough in numbers now to be within the regular population. Nurses are leaving, some to retire and others to change jobs. I think we are all feeling this underlying restlessness, the kind that make you think that a change of scenery might help. I think this is universal right now, not something you can get away from. We are all trying to get through it in our own ways, and many are leaving.

On one hand, the return to regular ICU and regular ICU patients is everything I have hoped for in a year. There is nothing like a patient with good old-fashioned alcohol withdrawal, or GI bleed, or a rotting limb, to quickly bring me back to the reality of my old role.

But on the other hand, I feel like a baby learning to walk. I feel cautious, unsteady, and untrusting of the world around me. I keep waiting for another shoe to drop or for something terrible to happen. I feel an insidious hum in the air, like the charged sensation seconds before the starting gun is fired in a footrace; I wonder when the waiting hum will end.

In one year, I took care of only four humans who were *not* critically ill with COVID. Three of those four came to me in the final week before the COVID unit was torn down. I have not begun to fully process my year within those walls. I doubt that my coworkers have either. I doubt that many in healthcare have; I am trying.

Just as the hospital is starting to work toward normal, so is the rest of society. In some ways, this is harder than the hospital's transition. People outside are so ready to start over, and that, too, is hard. Again, I liken the feeling to what a soldier must experience, coming home to a country that largely wants to move on, one that did not live this experience firsthand, one that did not have direct skin in the game.

I cannot participate in the vaccine discussion for long. I cannot explain to a layperson how, after seeing everything we saw, I honestly wouldn't care if I grew a third leg or was trackable from some satellite in outer space following that injection. I'd have let them shoot me with straight tequila, and I'd have accepted the shot with a smile just to avoid the possibility of being a Jack myself. No one fully understands that. And no statistic is going to change that for me. I am skewed, and I know it. But I am skewed by having seen the horrible, slow, fucking-heart-wrenching death for a year. And logic, which feels cold and alien in comparison, cannot undo that. Only time, safety, and the solidarity I share with other healthcare workers will bring me peace someday.

It is now June of 2021. I worked a night shift last night. We took a critically ill admission from the ER, one that went to surgery emergently and arrived to the floor in the middle of the night. Our hospital guidelines are only granting one visitor per patient at this time, so I was surprised to find four sets of eyes looking up expectantly when I entered the quiet waiting room at 4:00 a.m. A family. When I was asked later how I could be so cheerful in the middle of a twelve-hour night shift, I thought of this family. It hit me as I mulled it over—this was the first family I had seen face-to-face in over fifteen months. The first family that was not here to watch their loved one die from COVID. The first family that I got to give good news to, to reassure in person, to make smile. And those smiles were genuine. Finally. They were not the strained façade of someone trying to hold it together. It was the first family I have seen that I did not have to put into PPE. And it was an odd and wonderful feeling, to finally be able to comfort a family again.

In some ways, I am healing. In others, I am trapped in 2020. Since I finished writing this book, another hundred thousand Americans have died. That's a hundred thousand more stories of Jack: countless breaths, and too many final breaths. But despite that number, things are finally starting to look positive, like we may have a true end in sight.

I have been vaccinated for six months now. The number of vaccinated people is rising, and with that, the numbers of infected here have fallen dramatically. I have not seen one fully vaccinated human sick with COVID in the ICU. To me, this is everything we have prayed for; it is our chance to beat this, to find a way to truly move forward.

We, as a society, are starting to get back to "normal." This is a weird, mixed-up feeling. All I want is to feel normal again. I want to go into a store without thinking about masks or viruses. I want to go to work and not see their upside-down bodies in my mind, or the leftover airflow units in the rooms, the echoes of COVID in everything I do. I want to be able to put my respirator away and never need to use it again. I want Jack to leave the periphery of my mind, and to find his place in my stories. And slowly, I feel like that is happening.

But I feel different from how I did fifteen months ago, before the pandemic. It feels like my soul has been cracked into pieces, and it is slow work putting these pieces back together. The cracks are still visible, and I feel fragile and exposed. Time is helping. Baby steps into regular life are helping. Writing this out is helping. ICU nurses do not like to feel broken. We are supposed to be the ones healing others, not the ones who need healing. This year was a lesson in letting go—in accepting that sometimes all you can do is tread water and get through things with gritted teeth and fervent prayers.

I still feel best when I am in the trees. I listen to the shrieks of my children exploring and discovering, and everything feels right in the world. God and I are still talking often, and He is with me in the lush green leaves, bringing me solace. He gives me hope that this mixed, waiting feeling is temporary and that better things are yet to come.

I know now that no matter what happens in this life, we are not alone. People are capable of amazing things, and when things go sideways and shit hits the fan, I am reminded to look for the helpers and to make choices with love. Because that is all that matters. At the end of all of this, that is what I want to look back on and be proud of: that if I did one thing with my life, it was to give and speak and spread love; that if I can teach my children one thing, it is to love people. Love is what got me into the COVID ICU, and love will slowly get me out.

Jack, you've taught me so much. Let's keep healing together.

Everybody just breathe.

DISCUSSION QUESTIONS

Being a healthcare worker during a pandemic was a marathon of emotions, and I honestly have not even begun to tap into the depths of everything I have buried this past year. I know I am not alone in this, and I hope that me sharing my story can help others share their own.

With the help of both my coworker and a counselor friend of mine, we created some discussion questions to attempt to get some of this emotional processing started. These can be done alone, or in a group.

1. Let's talk about fear. Amanda thinks fear can be good, healthy, and even protective. Do you agree?

   a. What fears did you face during the pandemic?
   b. Are those fears still impacting you today?

2. If you are a healthcare worker, in what ways have you been affected by COVID that your nonmedical friends and family have not experienced?

   a. Has your perception of your career changed?

    b. Were there times when you felt your life was unrelatable to your loved ones?
Why or why not?

3. Amanda began one essay with the sentences, "Family time. So much family time." We were home with our families for months, but we were also distant from many other people.

    a. How did you keep human connections with people you couldn't be physically present for?

    b. Did constantly being home with your family change those relationships for you as it did for Amanda?

    c. How has COVID impacted your feelings about the broader society we live in?

4. Why do you think Amanda chose to include her children in this narrative?

    a. Do you think the pandemic will have a lasting impact on today's youth?

    b. What lessons should be taught about this event in history to future generations?

5. Faith was an important part of Amanda's journey. She also found great comfort in nature. What helped anchor you this year?

6. Nurses are depicted as story keepers in this book. Do you think it's important to remember patients' stories, even if privacy laws prevent people from knowing them? Why or why not?

7. Did this book change any of your impressions about the pandemic?
   a. If so, which? If not, why not?
   b. Did this book impact any of your beliefs about healthcare?

8. Did COVID have any silver linings? Did you discover any unexpected joys or lessons during the year the world shut down?

Created with help from Lydia Lucca, RN, BSN, and Andrea Richison, M.Ed. School Counseling

ACKNOWLEDGMENTS

When you accidentally become an author, you fall into this world of moving parts that turn your story from just a bunch of words into something real, something you can hold. The people that make this happen are incredible.

To my editor, Kerry . . . *thank you* does not cut it. You took my lived experience and my raw emotion and somehow managed to get it all onto paper. You honestly helped me begin to heal.

To Lily, Hanna, and Laurie, my publisher and project managers, and to Dan, my designer . . . your support and encouragement was infectious. You saw what I was trying to convey even better than I could and allowed me to be me throughout it all—thank you.

To Tanya, Erin, Lydia, Natalie, Vanessa, and all my fellow COVID Unit volunteers . . . your teamwork and sweat and tears and fucking heart represent everything I love about this profession. I am honored to have lived this with you and would say yes again.

To my family. To my husband, Collin, you have always challenged me to succeed and cheered me on throughout this process. Thank you for your unconditional encouragement. I love you more than I can write in words, and you and I both know that is saying something. To our kids, Sammy and Lewie, you brought the comic relief for this year, and showed us how incredibly resilient children can be. You were the light in the darkness of this pandemic, and I am so happy to be your mom. You are my greatest accomplishment.

To the rest of my village . . . my parents, my classmates, my moms' group, my best friends (Erin, Melissa, and Paula from heaven), thank you, always.

And especially to my grandpa James Spainhour. Without your amazing support, this dream would never have come true. Thank you so much for this.

ABOUT THE AUTHOR

Amanda Vancene Peterson has always known she wanted to be a nurse. "It's in my blood," she jokes, referencing her status as a third-generation healthcare worker. Amanda's career spans over fifteen years, thirteen of which have been spent in a Minnesota ICU. When Amanda is not caring for patients, she enjoys singing, reading, disappearing into nature, and cooking healthy food her children hate. She lives in Hudson, Wisconsin, with her husband, two kids, and two English bulldogs, Smokey and Pickles.